DOUBLE TAKE
Two sides One story

The Queen's Pirates

DEREK PARKER

For the youngest Lethbridge

This story is based, as much as possible, on primary source material - the words and pictures of the people that witnessed the events described. Whilst it is not possible to know the exact thoughts, feelings and motives of all the people involved, the book aims to give an insight into the experience of the events, based on the available evidence.

Scholastic Children's Books
Commonwealth House, 1–19 New Oxford Street,
London, WC1A 1NU, UK
A division of Scholastic Ltd
London ~ New York ~ Toronto ~ Sydney ~ Auckland
Mexico City ~ New Delhi ~ Hong Kong

Published in the UK by Scholastic Ltd, 2004

ISBN 0 439 96312 5

Printed and bound by Nørhaven Paperback A/S, Denmark

Cover image supplied by Hulton Archive/Getty Images

2 4 6 8 10 9 7 5 3 1

The right of Derek Parker to be identified as the author of this work has been asserted by him in accordance with the Copyright, Designs and Patents Act, 1988.

Contents

Prologue

GOLD. BOTH MEN LOVED GOLD.

Francis Drake found it in the holds of the Spanish ships he captured. His quick little English ships sailed in under the high wooden walls of the great galleons, and he leaped on board with his men, frequently offering the defeated captains a glass of wine and a good meal before sending them on their way with their treasure safely stored on board his own ship. Then Drake would delight Queen Elizabeth by bringing her a share of the booty.

Walter Ralegh also took his share of Spanish gold. Although he rarely went to sea himself, he would send his own ships out, crewed by pirates. He too enjoyed the smile of the Queen when they returned with bars of Spanish gold, silver and precious jewels – almost as much as he enjoyed spending this wealth on the magnificent silver armour he wore at court and the pearls he wore in his ears.

The two men were very different. Ralegh came from a noble family, was well educated, bookish, a poet with a love of adventure but few chances of enjoying it. He questioned everything, even religion – a dangerous thing to do in the sixteenth century. He had no talent for making himself popular, and made enemies all too easily. Drake, on the other hand, came from nowhere, his firmly Protestant family poor and obscure. He dashed into battle unquestioningly. It wasn't his business to question orders. He thought nothing of personal danger and was adored by his crew, and by the black slave he freed and made his personal servant.

Both men were ruled by love of the same things: gold, England, and their Queen. Both became famous in their own time, Drake as a great sailor and explorer, Ralegh as an organizer, a planner of ambitious journeys of exploration. But at the same time, everyone knew that they were pirates – Queen Elizabeth's pirates.

Drake

The Master of the *Judith*

1538 – 1569

ONE YEAR HE WAS the captain of a small boat, bobbing about on the treacherous waters of the English Channel, carrying cargoes of coal or iron from one port to another, the next he was ashore on the coast of Africa, facing a crowd of angry natives armed with poisoned arrows. It was all very sudden, and unexpected, and exciting. But so was the whole life of Francis Drake.

Famous men don't always come from famous families. Drake was born into a farming family in the little village of Crowndale, near Tavistock in Devonshire. No one knows the precise year of his birth, but it was probably 1538 or 1539.

When Francis was about ten years old, his father, Edmund Drake, stole a horse and used it to hold up and rob an innocent traveller. He was caught and found guilty of highway robbery, but before he could be put in gaol, he fled from Devon to Kent with his wife and children (altogether he had 13 sons). Their new home was a hulk, an old ruined ship lying on the bank of the river Medway. Though not well educated, Edmund could read, and scraped together a living reading prayers to the men of the Navy.

Most of Francis's brothers – those that hadn't died in childhood – became seamen. Children started work at an early age in the sixteenth century, and almost as soon as the Drake family reached Kent, young Francis became apprentice to the master of a small ship. The ship carried different cargoes from port to port around the coast of the Westcountry, and sometimes across the Channel to the Spanish Netherlands (Belgium and Holland) and France. In the stuffy cabin of a small boat bouncing and plunging in the storms of the Channel, Francis found out how uncomfortable life at sea could be. But from the moment he set foot on deck, Francis loved the sea and by the time he reached his twenties he had become a real seaman. He had learned all about setting sails, steering a course, coping with high winds and stormy seas, and navigating in and out of the ports along the south coast of England.

The old captain became so fond of his young apprentice that he left him the ship when he died. So while still a young man Francis was not only an experienced sailor, but owned his own ship, which he continued to use to carry any small cargoes he could get hold of – iron, coal, leather and skins. He also had another job as a pilot. If a captain of a ship was unfamiliar with the way into a port there was a danger that he might run his craft onto a sandbank or rocks just below the surface of the water so he would employ someone who knew the coast well – a pilot – to guide him. Drake hired himself out and was soon making good money.

We don't know where Francis Drake lived during the 10 or 12 years that he owned and sailed his own small ship, but he loved the Westcountry, where he had been born, and soon settled in Plymouth, one of the great ports of southern England. He didn't live in luxury – he wasn't a wealthy man – but he lived in more comfort than some, whose mean, damp, smelly thatched cottages were uncomfortable and unhealthy. By the time Drake reached his early twenties he had bought his own house.

In 1563 Drake's distant relatives, the brothers William and John Hawkins, who owned several ships that sailed out of Plymouth, were looking for a purser. The purser looked after affairs on a ship on behalf of its owner, making sure that cargoes were properly loaded, seeing that the crew was paid, and generally keeping everything in order. The problem was that to do this, a purser needed to be able to read and write, and few sixteenth-century seamen were literate. When the Hawkins brothers found out that Drake had been taught reading and writing by his father, they offered him the job.

On his first long voyage, to north-east Spain, Drake did the job so well that three years later, in 1566, John

Hawkins asked the young man to sail with him on an expedition to the Caribbean. Drake was only too happy to rent his own little ship to another captain, and accept the invitation to sail to the Spanish Main.

These very words – "Spanish Main" – conjured up images of pirates and buried treasure. After Christopher Columbus had made his great voyage of discovery for Spain in 1492, the Spaniards believed that the Caribbean Sea, the great stretch of water north of the coasts of Colombia and Venezuela and south of the islands of Cuba, Santo Domingo and Puerto Rico, belonged to them. From Santo Domingo they sent out expeditions to Mexico and Peru, and soon fleets of ships were carrying rich cargoes of silver and gold back to Spain from "the Spanish Main", as the English called the whole area.

The settlers in the Spanish colonies there needed slaves who could work for them carrying heavy loads and loading ships – and the less they had to pay the labourers, or pay for the purchase of the slaves, the better. But where was this cheap labour to come from? The settlers' thoughts turned to Africa, and thus the terrible "slave trade" began. Ships from Europe would sail to the coast of Africa where armed men would go ashore and simply steal away young men, women and children from the villages. Chained hand and foot, they would be packed into the dark holds of the ships, given just enough food and water to keep them alive on the rough crossing, and sold to land-owners in the West Indies.

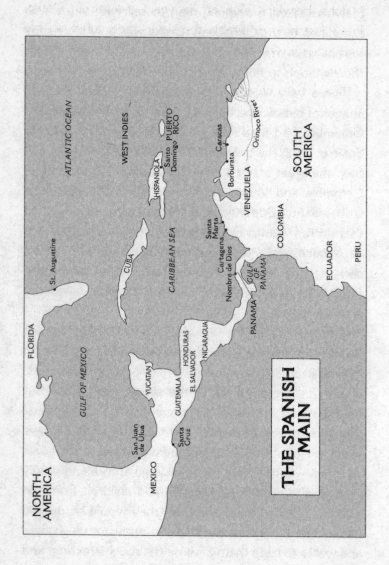

John Hawkins, five or six years older than Drake, knew just how profitable the slave trade could be. He was a pirate who dealt not in gold, but in human beings. Between 1562 and 1565 he led two expeditions to Africa, where he captured the natives, carried them to the West Indies, and exchanged them not for money, but for spices, sugar and drugs. In the sixteenth century nobody thought this was anything but an honest way of making money – Queen Elizabeth herself put cash into Hawkins's expeditions, as did several prominent London merchants. When some of the Spanish colonists were reluctant to trade with Hawkins (the Spanish government would rather they bought slaves from a Spanish ship than an English one) he just threatened them with his guns until they gave in. He took goods and treasure back to England, where the Queen – who had lent him one of her ships – was delighted when the money she had given him was returned, together with a very large profit.

When Drake received Hawkins's invitation to sail as an officer under the command of John Lovell, one of his captains, he accepted without hesitation. We don't know what he felt about the slave trade, attitudes to human rights and dignity were very different in the sixteenth century from today, but even if he felt pity for the human cargo, he had his way to make in the world, and he wanted adventure. So, on 9 November 1566 he set sail.

Lovell travelled first to Cape Verde in Senegal, where he seized a Portuguese vessel laden with slaves and ivory.

He came across four more Spanish slave ships on the way to the West Indies. He boarded them, took the slaves and sold them – with some difficulty – for £150 each. Though the Spanish colonists needed slaves, they were becoming increasingly annoyed that the English were getting in ahead of Spanish captains and making a profit that should have gone to them. (In fact, at several settlements Lovell was simply refused a licence to sell his slaves and actually gave 90 of them away, hoping that he could return later and force the Spanish to pay).

It was a rather disappointing voyage and the profits were small. In 1567, however, Drake was on the seas once again, in a fleet of six of Hawkins's ships, two of which – the *Jesus of Lubeck* and the smaller *Minion* – were warships. This time Drake was under the command of Hawkins himself, on the *Jesus*. The Queen once more put money into the venture, and so did some of her leading courtiers, including her chief minister William Cecil, later Lord Burghley. Publicly, the Queen assured King Philip of Spain that Hawkins would behave himself, and not interfere with Spanish interests overseas by selling slaves under the noses of Spanish captains. He would not even visit the West Indies, she promised. But Hawkins and his friends were pirates, and took little notice of the Queen's words – they knew perfectly well that she was just trying to keep King Philip sweet, and did not mean them to honour her promises. The Queen knew she would get away with these false promises because it was all part of the political game. There were other robbers on the high seas, called privateers. Privateers sailed with official permission from the government. They carried a "letter of marque", which allowed them to fire on enemy ships and to capture any merchant ships that might have valuable cargoes. Pirates did exactly the same thing, but without permission from the Crown. They were described as "sea-robbers". There was little difference between pirates and privateers, but when pirates came back to port with their ships full of treasure, and there were complaints from the country (usually Spain) to which it belonged, the Queen had the perfect excuse: they didn't carry her "letter of marque", and she knew nothing about their activities. Or so she said. Meanwhile, a good share of the treasure usually found its way into the royal coffers.

The fleet left Plymouth on 2 October, crewed by over 400 men. It immediately ran into a four-day storm so furious that Hawkins called the crew of the *Jesus* together to pray for deliverance. The *Jesus* had once been a fine ship, but she was now old and not at all safe. It took all the energy of the men to pump out the water that had got on board just to keep her afloat. This was Drake's first experience of a really rough Atlantic storm. It eventually passed without any ships actually sinking, and the pirates went on to the Canary Islands, then to the coast of west Africa. There Hawkins went ashore and stormed into a native village to capture men, women and children to be sold into slavery. This time, however, the natives were prepared. They fought back and Hawkins and 20 of his men were wounded by poisoned arrows. Eight of them died. Disappointed and angry, Hawkins sailed away. Almost immediately he ran into a Portuguese ship, the *Gratia Dei*. He ordered an attack, took her without difficulty, and put an English crew on board with Drake in command – his first big responsibility as master of a full-sized ship.

Six more Portuguese ships were seized near Cape Roxo, off the coast of what is now Senegal, and their cargoes of slaves were taken, but an attack on the settlement of Cacheo, not far away, was unsuccessful. Things improved at the island of Conga, in Sierra Leone, where Hawkins took advantage of a quarrel between two tribes and with the help of one of them captured 250 slaves from the other. Only a few of his men were killed or injured (although two men were drowned when their small boat was rammed by a hippopotamus). The holds were once more packed with slaves, chained to one another in airless holds with little food and water.

For the white men on deck, things were looking good. Hawkins decided to make for Dominica, one of the Windward Islands in the West Indies. From there he would sail back to Borburata, about 100 km west of Caracas in Venezuela, where he hoped to do business. Drake went on ahead of his commander on the *Judith*, and arrived alone at Rio de la Hacha, a pearl-fishing and mining town west of Borburata. He sent the Governor a request that he might come ashore, re-fill his water casks, and sell a few slaves. The Governor, Miguel de Castellanos, refused permission, so Drake sent a cannon shot clear through his house. This was a pretty rash action for a young man in his first command; but by now he had learned from Hawkins that when difficulties arose the best way of solving them was by force.

Hawkins probably approved of Drake's actions, but when he arrived some days later, he apologized to the Governor for Drake's ungentlemanly behaviour, hoping that the apology would make it easier for him to sell some of his slaves in the town. When Castellanos refused him a licence, Hawkins lost his temper and decided to teach him a lesson. He landed 200 troops and captured the town.

Despite the attack Castellanos still refused to grant a licence, and began burning the countryside around the town so that Hawkins could not seize the crops. The Englishman replied by setting fire to 20 houses, including Castellanos's own. The tit-for-tat quarrel continued until one of the men of the town turned traitor and showed Hawkins where the Spaniards had hidden their gold and treasure. This proved a better argument than guns and swords. The townspeople, terrified at the prospect of losing everything they owned, gave way and bought over 200 slaves from Hawkins, as well as paying some ransom for their property – in reality they were simply paying the English to go away and leave them alone.

Well contented, the English fleet sailed on. At Santa Marta, in Colombia, Hawkins sold more slaves, then decided to set sail for home with the few remaining Africans and over £13,000 in gold, silver and jewellery. Off the coast of Cuba a tremendous storm blew up, and once again the *Jesus* was almost lost – the planks of her hull *"did open and shut with every sea"*, as one of the sailors said. Fish swam in the water sloshing about inside the ship's hull. Hard work at the pumps and patching the holes in the ship's side saved her, and the fleet limped on to San Juan de Ulua, near Santa Cruz. There, to their surprise they were welcomed by a little procession of boats carrying the deputy Governor of Santa Cruz, Martin de Marçana, and its Treasurer, Francisco de Bustamante. These gentlemen were horrified when they got near enough to the *Jesus* to see her tattered English royal flag. They had thought they were greeting a flotilla of Spanish ships bringing the new Viceroy of Mexico, Don Martin Enriques.

After a hasty discussion, the Deputy Governor and the Treasurer continued to Hawkins's flagship, where he explained that he had only entered the port to repair his ships. They agreed to let him into the harbour, and he started tidying up the damage done to his ships in the recent storm. Hawkins "invited" the Treasurer and Deputy Governor to remain on board as he sailed into the anchorage and moored his ships.

This was on 15 September 1568. Two days later, the expected Spanish flotilla arrived – 13 ships, two of them warships and 11 more fully armed. This meant trouble. By Spanish law, Hawkins had no right to be in the Gulf of Mexico. It was the duty of the Spanish viceroy, Enriques, to destroy his ships. The Spanish fleet had larger guns than Hawkins, and more of them. Drake, on the *Judith*, must have felt particularly at risk – she was a tiny vessel.

Hawkins knew that attack was certain, and ordered most of his men ashore, where they captured the guns that protected the town. Using these guns, Hawkins hoped to keep the Spanish flotilla out of the harbour, but it would mean a battle, and the Queen, back in London, would not be happy to have to explain to the King of Spain that one of her captains had entered Spanish waters without permission and then fired on one of his viceroys.

Don Martin Enriques wanted to avoid a battle just as much as Hawkins did. It was his duty to fight the British, who had been given no reason to occupy the town, but he did not want to risk losing a battle, and perhaps several ships. Eventually he decided that Hawkins should be allowed to complete the repairs to his ships, as long as he handed back the Spanish guns and promised no violence. The Spanish vessels slid into the anchorage and tied up next to the English ones. Drake and the rest of the crew exchanged a few friendly words with the Spanish seamen.

But Enriques was preparing a surprise. He smuggled 150 armed men on to his biggest merchant ship, next to the *Minion*. The next thing the Englishmen knew was that Spanish soldiers were climbing over the side of the *Minion*, to the accompaniment of Spanish trumpets signalling the attack. The sound of Hawkins's own trumpeter quickly followed, and Hawkins was heard to cry: *"God and St George! Upon these traitorous villains, and rescue the* Minion! *I trust in God the day shall be ours!"*

A deafening roar of cannon split the air as the Spanish fired on the English ships from only a few metres away. Their fire was returned, the English concentrating their shot on the two most heavily armed Spanish ships. One was almost immediately holed and sunk, the second caught fire. Both were put out of action. But the guns on shore were also at work, and the *Angel*, the *Swallow*, the *Gratia Dei* and the captured Portuguese ship were disabled. Drake had moved the *Judith* out of danger – she was almost completely unarmed, and there was little he could do to help Hawkins, who, planning a careful retreat, signalled that Drake should bring the *Judith* in. He did so, and some stores, a little treasure and a number of men were hastily taken off the *Jesus* under the fire of the guns and placed aboard the *Judith*.

Then came a new danger: a fire-ship, perhaps the most fearful weapon of war at sea. One of the Spanish ships had been set on fire and it was heading directly towards the damaged *Jesus*. When it reached the English ship, the fire was sure to take hold and there would be no chance of putting it out. Hawkins and as many men as could follow him leaped from the deck of the *Jesus* on to the little *Minion*. Others, like the cabin-boy Paul

Hawkins, Hawkins's nephew and page, were too afraid to jump. He was last seen standing on the deck of the *Jesus*, a golden goblet and plates sparkling with precious stones clasped in his arms.

When the Spanish guns fell silent at nightfall both the *Minion* and the *Judith* were out at sea, desperately overcrowded, facing the prospect of a difficult voyage home through bad weather. The following morning, when Hawkins looked out from the deck of the *Minion*, there was no sign of the *Judith*. Hawkins always believed that Drake deserted his commander at San Juan de Ulua. Drake, he later wrote, *"forsook us in our great misery"*.

His action has never been fully explained. He was certainly no coward, but what excuse was there? If Drake ever said anything on the subject, his words have been lost. The most likely explanation is that he was eager to get his overcrowded vessel safely home through the rough Atlantic storms – which indeed he did, landing at Plymouth on 20 January 1569.

Hawkins also successfully returned, though he and his men endured great misery. With nowhere near enough food to go round, they ate the parrots they had been bringing home to sell, and rats from the holds. They even, finally, chewed pieces of leather to comfort their empty stomachs.

The fate of the 200 or 300 men left in the hands of the Spaniards was even worse. Many were tortured, others were left to rot in prison or were burned at the stake. The treasure in the hold of the *Minion* was little comfort to Hawkins, although it was just enough to cover the expenses of the failed expedition. After he had stepped ashore at Penzance on 25 January, he wrote to William Cecil that *"if I should write of all our calamities I am sure a volume as great as the Bible will scantly suffice."* (That is, he would need a book as long as the Bible to tell of all their misfortunes).

Drake's first taste of command had not been a success and the Hawkins brothers now regarded him as little better than a traitor. But he had learned one lesson he would never forget – to hate the Spanish passionately. A firm Protestant, he had always stood against their Catholicism. Now he hated them for their deceit – promising Hawkins's ships safe passage when they had completed their repairs, but instead boarding and destroying them. Finally, he hated Spain for the slaughter of his friends and shipmates, and the relentless cruelty to those who had been captured.

Young Ralegh goes to War

1552 – 1572

IN 1552, when Drake was a boy of 12 and probably still living with his father in the dirt and cold and discomfort of the old hulk in Kent, a child who was to become equally famous was born under very different circumstances. He was Walter Ralegh. Until recently it was usual to spell that name "Raleigh", though Walter never spelt it that way. He spelt it many different ways, "Rawley", "Raulie", "Rawlegh", "Rawlie", "Rawlighe", "Rawlye" and even "Rawleyghe", but he and his wife usually spelt it "Ralegh", and that is the way we shall spell it.

Walter Ralegh was not born rich, but he did come from an ancient and honourable family, one of the oldest in Devonshire. By the time of Walter's birth, the family had come down in the world. His father left the family home at Fardel Manor, near Cornwood – not far from

Plymouth – and went into the shipping business in Exmouth. He married three times, and his last wife, young Walter's mother, was Elizabeth Champernowne, who gave birth to Walter at a small house at Hayes, in the parish of East Budleigh, near the main road from Plymouth to Exeter.

Walter enjoyed a quiet childhood in the countryside and by the sea, but when he was 14 or 15 years old his mother's cousin, Henry Champernowne, decided to go on a crusade to France with 100 volunteers to help the Huguenots, Protestants who were being persecuted by the Catholic majority. Another Champernowne cousin was married to a highborn French Protestant, and as the situation worsened for the Huguenots, the Devonshire Champernownes decided to go to their aid. As most of the families of Devon and Cornwall had no enthusiasm for Catholicism there was no difficulty in mustering a small army. Walter went with them, and spent four years there.

The main quarrel between Catholics and Protestants in England had started when Queen Elizabeth's father, Henry VIII, was King, and the country was Catholic. Because the Pope refused him permission to divorce his first wife, Catherine of Aragon, so that he could marry Anne Boleyn, he set up the Protestant Church of England, and made himself head of it. During the 1530s the Catholic monasteries in England were destroyed, and Catholic priests outlawed. When Henry's daughter Mary came to the throne in 1553, she tried to reverse the situation and reinstated Catholicism as the "official" religion. Then, in 1554, Mary married the Catholic Prince Philip of Spain. She died childless after only two years of marriage, and her Protestant half-sister Elizabeth came to the throne in 1558. In the 1560s the English, now ruled by a Protestant Queen and largely very happy about it, were horrified to hear that King Philip (as he had become) was supporting the Catholics who were torturing, burning and killing thousands of Protestants in France and the Netherlands. Ralegh, a loyal Protestant, was happy to join Champernowne and his little army to help the oppressed Protestants in France.

We don't know what part he played in the battles that followed, but we do know that he learned a great deal about fighting. At first hand, he saw how attacks were planned and how defences were laid out. He saw deeds of bravery and cowardice, he saw extreme cruelty and death. And he found out about taking risks – for his cousin explained to him that if he was captured, he could expect no mercy from the French, and no rescue attempts by the English. Queen Elizabeth had decided to stay out of the dispute between the Huguenots and the Catholics in France, and had told the French ambassador that any Englishman fighting in France did so without her knowledge or permission. If he was captured, Walter would hang.

He was present at two battles between the Huguenots and the Catholics, and was almost killed in one, when the Huguenot fighters retreated, followed by a band of German Catholics who killed every prisoner they took. On another occasion he was one of a group of Huguenots who smoked some Catholics out of caves in Languedoc, where they had taken refuge. He later wrote:

> *We knew not how to enter by any ladder or engine, till at last, by certain bundles of lighted straw let down by an iron chain with a weighty stone in the midst, those that defended it were so smothered that they surrendered themselves, with their plate, money and other goods therein hidden, or they must have died like bees that are smoked out of their hives.*

As he grew into a young man, Ralegh saw plenty of the cruelty and horror of war. He got used to the idea of killing – though he hated the idea that the two sides that were fighting each other came mostly from the same country: "*The greatest and most grievous calamity that can come to any state is civil war,' he said; 'it is a misery more lamentable than can be described.*"

Walter Ralegh went to France as a boy. He came back to England as a young man.

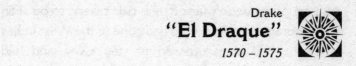

Drake
"El Draque"
1570 – 1575

As soon as Drake reached Plymouth and told William Hawkins about the tragic events at San Juan de Ulua, he was sent off to London with letters to the Queen describing Enriques's treachery and asking for permission to go out and attack Spanish shipping wherever they found it. Hawkins wanted revenge, although he was also keen to make some money to pay for the loss of his expensive ships and the treasure they had carried.

The Queen and her council were not sure what to do. Elizabeth was irritated by the fact that the Spanish had control of the West Indies, but she accepted that they probably had the right to be, since they had been the first to trade there. When Drake, Hawkins and other pirates began to attack Spanish shipping, ordinary people thought they were heroes – and the Queen was privately pleased. But if Drake and Hawkins set off to capture

Spanish ships on the Spanish Main, Spain was certain to retaliate and attack English ships in other parts of the world. And although it seemed that war between the two countries wasn't far off, she didn't want to be seen to encourage Hawkins, who had gone to the West Indies when he had been ordered to stay away, and had attacked Spanish and Portuguese ships for no other reason than greed.

Then there was this young man from Devon, Francis Drake, who was just as thirsty for revenge as Hawkins. He was supported by the people of Plymouth, many of whose husbands and sons and nephews were prisoners in Spain or had died at the hands of the Spanish.

The Queen decided that taking immediate revenge wasn't the right cause of action, and sent Drake away, discontented. Back home he discovered that John Hawkins's ship had finally managed to reach Plymouth, and he had complained bitterly to his brother about the young man's desertion. We don't know how Drake answered him, and we don't know much about what happened to him in the following months. He probably decided to lie low for a while and keep out of trouble. We do know that he got married in 1569, to a Cornishwoman, Mary Newman. They settled in a house in Notte-street in Plymouth, just below the fort that protected the town, and near the Barbican, the waterfront from which all vessels set sail. It was from here that Drake again set out for the West Indies in 1570. He used his own money to prepare two ships, the *Swan* and the *Dragon*, and recruited men to crew them. He probably promised them a share in whatever profits he could make from piracy, or maybe from the slave trade.

Plymouth men were keen to sail with him. He was not a hero yet but the Spanish were seen as Catholic devils over the water. Drake's Protestant countrymen thought that it was his right – almost a duty – to attack any Spanish ship and bring its treasure home, and anyone who was asked to join his crew was honoured to do so.

When Drake set off for the Caribbean, he was the first Englishman to do so simply as a pirate. His first voyage there as captain of his own ship, however, turned out to be more one of discovery than anything else. There is no evidence that he actually attacked any Spanish vessels or brought home any treasure. How he paid his crew is a mystery but he did come back with a lot of valuable information. For example he discovered the pathways by which Spanish mule-trains – groups of mules travelling one behind the other – brought the gold and silver mined in Bolivia, Mexico, Chile and Peru down through dense jungle to the little Panamanian town of Venta Cruces on the Chagres River, and then on down-river to the port of Nombre de Dios.

Nombre de Dios was the most important of all the Spanish bases in the Caribbean. Two *flotas*, or fleets, of vessels came every year from Europe and landed supplies there to be sent on to other Spanish settlements. The ships that brought them were then loaded with treasure for the return journey. Nombre de Dios was poorly protected, and there were very few Spanish ships in the area. The few soldiers who guarded the mule-trains that carried the treasure along tangled jungle pathways through hot and steamy forests were so exhausted by the simple effort of making the journey that they were in no fit state to fight. All that treasure was just asking to be stolen.

Drake wasn't quite ready for that though. In February 1571, he set out from Plymouth with just one ship, the *Swan*, to raise funds. It was an easy voyage to the Caribbean, and once there he captured no fewer than 12 large ships loaded with slaves and all manner of goods. This was the first opportunity Drake had to demonstrate that he was a much better seaman than any of the Spanish captains he encountered. He was simply better at taking advantage of the winds, manoeuvring his ship into the best position for firing his guns. From this time onwards his reputation as someone to be feared grew and grew.

Drake wanted all the space available on his own ship to store the treasure he meant to take. He didn't want to waste time arranging the sale of slaves when it was so much quicker and sometimes easier to capture Spanish treasure ships, so Drake would free the slaves, setting them ashore, and load everything of value from the captured ships into the hold of the *Swan*.

On 8 May he came across a large galleon carrying messages from the Caribbean to Philip of Spain. Its captain was killed and several of the crew were wounded during the fight, but Drake took the ship and everything of value on it, leaving the survivors on a desert island.

It was on this voyage that Drake discovered a little cove on the coast east of Nombre de Dios. It was *"a fine round bay of very safe harbour for all winds … having ten or twelve fathom water, more or less [about 18 metres], full of good fish, the soil also very fruitful,"* as one of his crew remembered. It was just the place to slip into and hide, if he was being chased by the Spaniards. If he needed to lay quiet for a while to repair his ship, he could stay safely for several weeks in Port Pheasant (he called it that *"by reason of the great store of those goodly fowls which he and his company did then daily kill and feed on in that place"*).

Drake sailed back to Plymouth with the *Swan* full of stolen merchandise. His first solo venture made him a large profit – more than Hawkins had made on his last three slaving voyages put together. And he had made his name famous in the Caribbean. Spanish officials in Panama wrote to King Philip complaining that "El Draque", as they called him (the nearest they could get to spelling and pronouncing his name), was so much in control of the whole coast around Nombre de Dios that their ships dare not approach it. Three expeditions had been sent to arrest him, but they could not find him – *"he has always had the luck to escape,"* they said. They asked the King to send two galleons to protect them from this remarkable pirate.

Back in Plymouth, Drake's crew praised his courage, his cunning, his coolness when in danger. He was a real hero, they said. The Hawkins brothers were impressed, and when he was ready to sail again, they agreed to forget their differences and lent him one of their large ships, the *Pasco*, which could carry 50 men and 12 guns. On 24 May 1572, Drake left Plymouth Sound again as her captain, with the *Swan* captained by his younger brother John (a second brother, Joseph, and a young nephew also sailed with them). The combined crew of 73 men were almost all in their twenties – Drake was the eldest of them, and he was only 34. The ships carried enough food for a year, plenty of weapons, and three pinnaces – small boats that were laid on the deck in pieces, to be quickly put together when needed for working in shallow water.

The crews and their commander were in high spirits. Drake's mind was on a great treasure trove – more gold than any English pirate had ever thought of stealing. His crew knew it, and were thinking of their share.

Once again Drake enjoyed an easy voyage to the Caribbean and on 12 July the two ships approached Port Pheasant. But when Drake went ashore, a nasty surprise awaited him. Nailed to a tree was a note that read:

Captain Drake, if you fortune [happen] to come to this port, make haste away, for the Spaniards which you had with you here last year betrayed this place, and have taken away all that you left here.

I departed from hence, this present 7 of July, 1572.
Your very loving friend, John Garret.

Drake knew Garret, who came from his native town, and trusted him. It was not often he made such a serious mistake as setting free prisoners who had information that could be used against him.

He left the safe harbour and sailed along the coast, capturing two Spanish ships along the way. There was no valuable cargo, but he set free the slaves he caught, *"that they might join themselves to their countrymen the cimarrons, and gain their liberty if they would"*. The cimarrons were outlaws, ex-slaves eager to revenge themselves on their former Spanish owners. They lived up in the thick forests of the mountains of Panama, attacking mule-trains when the opportunity arose. They weren't interested in gold, taking mainly food and wine. Drake thought it a good idea to get on the right side of them. It proved a very wise move.

At Nombre de Dios Drake and his men went ashore in small boats. They sailed in by moonlight and crept up to the group of guns that guarded the town. Only one man was on watch – and he ran away as soon as he saw them. Drake led his company on into the town.

The church bells began to ring in warning as they marched in, and Drake ordered his trumpeters and drummers to sound, hoping to frighten the townspeople. Shots rang out, and Drake was wounded in the leg. Nevertheless, the English triumphed easily as the defenders left their posts and ran for their lives. Drake now had to empty the town of treasure before reinforcements arrived. He made for the Governor's house, and there, according to one of his nephews who wrote about him years later found:

> ...*a pile of bars of silver, of (as near as we could guess) seventy foot in length, of ten foot in breadth, and twelve foot in height, piled up against the wall. Each bar was between thirty-five and forty pound in weight. At sight hereof our captain commanded that none of us should touch a bar of silver ... because there was in the King's treasure-house near the water's side more gold and jewels than all our four pinnaces could carry.*

They went down to the treasure-house and Drake ordered his men to break into it, but then:

> *His strength and sight and speech failed him, and he began to faint for want of blood, which, as we then perceived, had in great quantity issued [dripped] upon the sand out of a wound received in his leg ... whereby, though he felt some pain, yet he would not have it known to any till this, the blood having filled the very prints which his footsteps made, to the great dismay of all our company, who thought it not credible that one man should be able to spare so much blood and live.*

One of Drake's boots was actually full of blood. He had not shown any sign that he was injured, and tried to insist that the men carry on their attempt to break open the treasure-house – but they refused to obey him, bound up his leg, and carried him protesting back to the pinnaces. This intense loyalty, the crew putting the safety of their captain before the treasure, was an example of Drake's talent for making his men love him.

The ships made for the Bastimentos Islands, west of Nombre de Dios, where Drake and one or two other wounded men were nursed. He was looked after by the cimmerone Diego, his most loyal servant and friend.

As he convalesced he began to make plans for an attack on the shipping that lay at anchor at Cartagena, in Colombia, the most important port of the Spanish Main.

Recovered from his wound, on the night of 13 August, he slipped into the bay of Cartagena with two ships and three pinnaces. He boarded a Spanish vessel, which turned out to be guarded by only one man – the rest of the crew had gone ashore to watch a duel between two shipmates. The guard told Drake that the rest of the ships in the port lay closer in, under the protection of a stone tower and guns on the island of Getsemani. Drake decided that it would be too dangerous to attack. He boarded another ship, set her on fire – just to advertise the fact that he had been there – then sailed out to sea again.

It was at this time that he began to make friends with the cimarrons, and use this alliance to his own advantage. It was a new idea. No Englishman had thought of working with black men before. If anyone thought of them at all, it was as slaves, or men who could be captured and sold as slaves, but Drake realized that they could be useful allies, and with Diego as a close friend came to trust them as much as he trusted his Devonshire crew. He was never heard to talk to any of them except in a friendly and polite way and no one ever saw a hint of racial prejudice in him. The Spaniards were surprised and angry. *"This league between the English and the Negroes is very detrimental to this kingdom,"* wrote one of King Philip's representatives, *"because being so acquainted with the region and so expert in the bush, the Negroes will show them methods and means to accomplish any evil design they may wish to carry out."*

While he was at sea keeping a lookout for more Spanish ships to plunder, Drake's brother John attempted a little piracy of his own. He boarded a Spanish ship armed only with a broken sword and a fishing spear. He was shot in the stomach, and lived only long enough to dictate a farewell message to his young wife back in Plymouth. When Drake returned to Port Pheasant, having captured a Spanish vessel and taken enough food to feed his ship's company on the voyage back to England, he heard not only of John's death, but also that of his other brother, Joseph. The yellow fever, brought to the area by the slaves, had taken hold of the crew and went on to kill almost half of the men. They renamed the place Slaughter Island.

Drake had had enough for the time being, and so had his crew. They had been away long enough from their families and they did not want to die of "yellow-jack". They believed that if they put to sea, the fever could be controlled. They all wanted to go home.

But as preparations were almost complete, one of the cimarrons reported that the winter *flota* had arrived at Nombre de Dios. Over the next few weeks the treasure that it was to carry back to Spain would be loaded on to the ships. Drake could not resist the thought of one final effort to get his hands on a really rich hoard of treasure.

Once they heard about the treasure train, he easily persuaded his remaining crew to postpone their voyage home. He and 18 of the strongest and healthiest of his men, with another Plymouth man, John Oxenham, as his second-in-command, set out from Slaughter Island with a number of cimarrons. After a week's tiring journey through the tangled and steamy rainforest, they reached a high hill above Panama. There Drake climbed an enormous tree and saw for the first time the vast Pacific Ocean stretching to a far horizon. His nephew tells us that at that moment he *"besought Almighty God of His goodness to give him life and leave to sail once in an English ship in that sea"* – believing that even more treasure was to be found in an ocean so far completely dominated by Spain.

They camped in the safety of the forest, and sent a cimarron to gather information. He returned with the news that the Treasurer of Lima was about to leave Panama for Nombre de Dios with a mule-train carrying a great deal of gold. Two more would follow, carrying silver. Drake laid a careful ambush, but just as they were about to attack the train, one of his men, who had drunk too much brandy, staggered out in full view of the Spanish, and the mule-train turned back. Drake knew they would immediately report his position, and that the Spanish would soon be hot on his heels. He and his men trudged back to their ships, disheartened and exhausted – except for the cimarrons however, who not only carried the provisions but sometimes their exhausted white companions too. Without them, the whole party might well have died.

Drake was undecided as to what to do next, but fate dealt him a lucky hand. By happy chance he came across a French ship, a Huguenot privateering vessel commanded by Guillaume Le Testu, an experienced seaman with whom Drake quickly made friends. The two crews would join together to attack the treasure-train at the Campos River, as it approached Nombre de Dios. They would share the gold and silver, half and half.

On 31 March 1573 a French and English force gathered so close to the town that they could hear men at work on the defences. They waited. Early the following morning the cimarron spies reported the approach of almost 200 mules loaded with treasure, guarded by 45 soldiers. However they also reported that the soldiers seemed exhausted and were poorly armed, some of them actually barefoot.

The pirates fell on them, most fled, and the rest were quickly defeated. The only serious casualty was Captain La Testu, who was shot in the stomach, and later died. When the mules were unloaded, the treasure was so heavy that it was impossible to carry all of it away. The pirates buried 15 tons of silver, hoping to recover it later, and carried most of the gold back towards their ships. But when they reached the anchorage, they saw, instead of their own craft, seven armed Spanish ships.

What had happened to the English ships? They had obviously not been captured; if there had been a fight there would be signs of it – the bodies of the slain for instance so Drake supposed they must be somewhere a little further along the coast. He couldn't stay on land – he knew the Spaniards must be close behind – so he ordered his men to make a small raft, and on it he, one of his English crewmen, and two Frenchmen set out to round the coast under the noses of the Spanish. *"God willing,"* he told the rest, *"he would by one means or another get them all abroad [away], in despite of all the Spaniards in the Indies."* They must have doubted even their great leader as they watched the rough raft make off, swamped by the waves, beneath which sharks waited for a meal.

The raft eventually came in sight of the two English vessels and the pinnaces. The raft fell to pieces as it landed, and Drake and his men made their way to the spot where the pinnaces were moored. The crew was astonished to see the four men approach them and even more startled to realize that one of them was their commander. Clearly there had been a disaster. Then Drake pulled out from under his clothing a nugget of Spanish gold, and they were greatly reassured.

The rest of the crew was picked up, and the treasure that they had been carefully guarding was equally divided. The French ship sailed away, and Drake returned to Plymouth with his booty. Behind him, he left a name that had become synonymous with courage – and luck.

He sailed into Plymouth Sound on 9 August 1573. It was a Sunday, and many of the townspeople were at worship in St Andrew's church. They left the preacher alone in the pulpit and rushed down to greet Drake and his crew – their husbands and brothers – home from the Spanish Main.

Despite the fact that Drake had returned with treasure the value of which amounted to one-fifth of the Queen's whole annual income – and she, of course, had her share – there was no open rejoicing at court when he presented himself in London. Elizabeth and Philip of Spain had been making some attempt to be friendly, and the Queen was eager not to anger the King too much. Drake was no fool, and completely understood the situation. He lay low for almost two years, until July 1575, when he was invited to lend his skill to Walter Devereux, the first Earl of Essex, then fighting rebels in Ireland. He commanded a small force that captured the Isle of Rathlin.

This battle was the scene of one of the most infamous slaughters of defenceless Irish civilians by English forces under Essex. Drake had nothing to do with this: he only organized the invasion and capture. He was always ready to fight when necessary, but never killed anyone needlessly. He was generous to his prisoners, and had gone out of his way to protect his Spanish captives from cimarrons who would have killed them. He did what was necessary to capture Rathlin, and continued for a while to guard the seas nearby, but there is no evidence that he played any further part in persecuting the Irish, and may well have been pleased to be able to turn his thoughts once more to the Caribbean – and particularly to the Pacific.

Friends with the Queen

1572 – 1582

RALEGH HAD NO SOONER returned unharmed from Champernowne's expedition to France, some time around the middle of 1572, than he travelled up to Oxford to study at Oriel College. It was a sudden change, from the heat and excitement of battle to the quiet of a university – but it was his decision. A young man of 18 was his own master, and Ralegh had a taste for books and learning. So while Drake was already on his first solo expedition to the West Indies, Ralegh settled down to study. He had made no money during his time with the army, and had very little in the way of possessions – he even had to borrow a gown from a fellow student (which he never returned).

He found university life dull after his French adventures. The students *"had nothing in the world to do, but when they had said their prayers at stated hours, to employ themselves in instructive studies,"* as a writer of the time put it. But at Oxford he had time to read and write for his own pleasure. He began to write poetry, which he went on doing until his death. If we had never heard of him as a great admiral, we would still recognize him as one of the best poets of his age.

While Drake was fighting the Irish rebels, Ralegh moved on from Oxford to London and the Middle Temple. This was one of the Inns of Chancery, where lawyers studied – and where young men went to finish their education, even if they didn't mean to be lawyers. It was during this time that he published his first poem, with lines that seem to foretell his future life as a famous but much-hated man: *"For whoso reaps renown above the rest. With heaps of hate shall surely be oppressed"*.

One of his friends at court – Sir Humphrey Gilbert, his half-brother, 16 years older than he, had been a personal servant of Queen Elizabeth before she came to the throne. Walter used this friendship to find his way into the court circle and to be introduced to some of the men it was worth knowing if a young man wanted to get on.

Where the money came from, we don't know, but in London he kept two servants, and dressed well enough to mix with those who were close to the Queen. When he first appeared at court, another relative, Adrian Gilbert, loaned him £60 with which he ordered clothes for himself and uniforms for his servants. (This does not sound much but one pound in 1550 would be worth

£240 today, so Ralegh actually spent the equivalent of £14,400 on his wardrobe!)

After a rather dull time of it at Oxford, he had some riotous times. He lived in Islington, not one of the more fashionable parts of London at the time. His servants often misbehaved, and so occasionally did he. *"His companions were boisterous blades* [noisy louts]", the historian John Aubrey wrote. There is a story that at an inn a fellow drinker upset Ralegh by talking too much and too loudly, so he joined the man's moustache to his beard with sealing wax – a good way of keeping him quiet. When, many years later, his son got drunk and behaved badly, he always made the excuse that his father had done the same thing before him.

It was in 1578 that Ralegh became a working pirate. He had heard tales about them since he was a child, and knew all about Francis Drake, who was beginning to make his name as a pirate (even if people didn't actually call him that). And now Sir Humphrey Gilbert was given a licence by the Queen *"to discover, search, find out and view such remote heathen and barbarous lands, countries and territories not actually possessed by any Christian prince or people"* and to put men ashore to build settlements and claim the land on behalf of England. What young man could resist the chance to join Gilbert when the invitation came?

As far as the public knew, the discovery of new lands

was the main purpose of the voyage. But in fact Gilbert and his associates were planning to make straight for Newfoundland, where Spanish, Portuguese and French fleets were fishing. The English would fall upon the defenceless fishing-boats, put armed crews on board – only one or two men would be necessary to force the unarmed fishermen to obey – and sail them to Holland, where they would sell the fish and the boats. Although the English Government could not publicly support such a venture, so many ministers and wealthy merchants were helping to pay for the expedition that the Government could be relied upon to turn a blind eye.

Gilbert and Ralegh began preparations at the Devonshire port of Dartmouth, fitting out ten ships, loading them with enough supplies to last for a whole year, and recruiting crews – 365 men in all. On 26 September 1578, Ralegh set sail as part of the fleet, as captain of the *Falcon*, a ship that the Queen herself had supplied. By the time he took his first command, Drake was an experienced seaman. In contrast, Ralegh was just a poet who had done some fighting in France. There were expert sailors on board who could take the ship wherever he wanted it to go, but Ralegh was an intelligent man who soon learned how to make the best use of wind and weather.

The high winds and rough seas that had often delayed Drake's voyages before they had properly started now delayed Ralegh and Gilbert, who had to wait in Plymouth Sound while the storm went on for several days. Three ships deserted the fleet, their crews vanishing ashore, and those who stayed on board were almost all sea-sick. A satirical poet, Thomas Churchyard, made fun of them:

And still a fulsome smell
Of pitch and tar they feel,
And when seasick (Got wet) they are,
About the ship they reel,
And stomach belcheth up
A dish that haddocks seek,
A bitter mess of sundry meats
A syrup green as leek.

The seven remaining vessels set sail on 19 November, but once more were beaten back – all except the *Falcon*. Ralegh was impatient to get going on this new adventure, and ordered his ship out into the Atlantic alone, determined, he said later, *"to do something worthy of honour"*.

Very soon he found himself in the middle of a group of Spanish ships off the Cape Verde islands. He challenged them but there were too many for him. Some of his crew were killed, and the Queen's ship, badly damaged, limped back to Plymouth. When she heard of the defeat Elizabeth ordered both Sir Humphrey and young Ralegh to settle down, stay at home, and keep out of trouble for a while.

Ralegh was furious at the Queen's orders. He was burning to go back to sea, to make his name and fortune, but to disobey the Queen was unthinkable so he let off steam in other ways. In February 1580 he and a friend, Sir Thomas Perrot, had a row and began to fight in a public place. They were both arrested and sent to prison. They were only released when they promised to keep the peace and *"demean themselves quietly* [behave themselves]*"*. Not long after Ralegh had been released he found himself behind bars again; this time for fighting with another man behind the tennis courts in Whitehall. Prison in the sixteenth century was not the same as it is today, though, especially if you were of noble birth and moved in courtly circles. Ralegh was allowed to invite friends to his cell, enjoy food brought in by his servants, take exercise outdoors when he wished, and spend quiet time writing; during his imprisonment he wrote several of his early poems.

The Queen had heard many stories about this hot-headed, handsome, clever young man, and not long after his release – to his surprise – she made him Esquire of the Body Extraordinary. The "Body Extraordinary" referred to the Queen although it was really a figure of speech. It was more or less just a title and Ralegh didn't actually have to do anything as Esquire. He was simply the courtier who represented those who had to guard the Queen.

However the appointment meant the Queen had noticed him, and that she thought him worth encouraging. Shortly afterwards – in the summer of 1580 – she sent him to command a force of 100 men in Ireland. She had always been determined to make Ireland a Protestant country; the Catholics, she thought, would be a danger to England. Many of the Irish were unhappy about this, and recently there had been trouble in the district of Munster, where in 1579 a troop of Spanish, French, Portuguese and English Catholics had landed to help the Catholic Irish fight the Protestant Queen of England.

Even people who admire Ralegh find it difficult to excuse his actions in Ireland, for there is no doubt that he was as cruel to the Irish rebels as anyone before or since. One of his first actions in Ireland was to order the hanging, drawing and quartering of an Englishman who had supported the Irish in their rebellion. Men sentenced to death in this way were often mercifully strangled; but to make an example of traitors Ralegh ordered that the sentence be carried out as intended. The man was hanged, but cut down while still alive, then his heart was torn out while he still breathed, and his body was chopped into quarters.

The cruelty continued. When 400 Spanish and Italian soldiers surrendered to Ralegh at Smerwick, on the west coast of Munster, he ordered the killing not only of the soldiers, but many of the men and women of the town. Two traitors were tortured to death, and hundreds of the people who were killed died slowly and painfully.

Once, when he was out riding, Ralegh came across an Irish peasant collecting thin willow branches, which were used to make halters for their horses. When he asked what the fellow wanted the wood for, the Irishman replied, *"to hang English churls* [peasants]*"*. *"Is it so?"* responded Ralegh. *"Well, they shall now serve for an Irish kerne* [a wild Irishman]*!"* and had him hanged on the spot.

Many Englishmen would have behaved the same way. One wrote that *"to kill an Irishman in Munster was thought no more of than to kill a mad dog"*. Ralegh wasn't forced to obey orders. He clearly believed that cruelty was necessary to make the Irish into good subjects of the Queen.

At the same time, Ralegh often showed great personal courage. One day, he and some companions were ambushed by a band of Irishmen and outnumbered ten to one. When one of his companions, Henry Moyle, fell off his horse and was about to be killed, Ralegh rode back and rescued him, single-handed. It was this kind of action, as well as his fearsome reputation as an executioner, that made his name; he was soon admired by the English as much as he was feared by the Irish.

By the end of 1581 the country was relatively quiet, and he had little to do. Soon afterwards he was recalled to London, where the Queen was delighted with him. But he did not make himself popular with the other courtiers: in the know-all way that so often annoyed people, he violently criticized the Englishmen with whom he had served in Ireland. The commanders, other than himself, were fools and *"the men are poor and miserable creatures"*, he said.

He also lectured the Queen's council about how affairs in Ireland should be managed. Instead of rampaging around the countryside killing every suspicious Irishman, the English soldiers should take care to make friends with those Irish who might be persuaded to take their side – often they suffered more from high local taxes and cruel landlords than from the English. The council was impressed, though the commanders in Ireland disliked the idea (but then, Ralegh had criticized them as inefficient fools).

The Queen thought his arguments were sensible (then again anything likely to save money was popular with her). It was at this time that she really got to know Ralegh personally. From the start, he went out of his way to persuade her to think of him not just as a subject, but also as a friend. There is a famous story that when she was walking and came to a muddy place, he took off his expensive cloak and laid it over the puddle so that she would not get her feet dirty. The tale itself may not be true, but it illustrates the gallantry with which he treated her. In any case, she always had an eye for a handsome man, and Ralegh's appearance and dress earned him her favour.

He was, Aubrey says, *"a tall, handsome and bold man"* and *"damnable proud"*. He was pale, with a clear complexion, shiny black hair and a curly beard, and eyes that seemed to look right to the heart of anyone he met.

His clothes (when, later, he could afford to spend money on them) were among the most gorgeous and costly of anyone's at the court, often made from cloth of silver and satin, his waistcoat sparkling with seed pearls and a number of brilliant rings on his fingers. When Ralegh was in the room, he was always the centre of attention. Like Drake, the one thing he never managed to get rid of was his Westcountry accent. Aubrey remembers that *"notwithstanding his so great mastership in style and his conversation with the learnedest and politest persons, yet he spake broad Devonshire to his dying day"* in a soft, sweet voice. (One of the Queen's pet names for him was "Warter", which was in imitation of his broad accent.)

As well as his pleasing appearance, Ralegh was intelligent and witty, and this appealed to the Queen. It is said that one day he took a diamond ring and cut on a window the words *"Fain would I climb, yet I fear to fall."* Whereupon the Queen took the ring and scratched underneath the words *"If thy heart fail thee, climb not at all"*.

This seemed to hint that if Ralegh did climb, he would be rewarded. The two shared a love of music, poetry and learning – Ralegh told the Queen that when he was on a long voyage at sea he spent much of the time studying, and that *"he carried always a trunk of books along with him"*. He hadn't so far made a really long voyage, and Elizabeth probably knew it, but she forgave that. The truth was that she was ready for a new admirer. The other male courtiers who had been close to her were growing middle-aged and plump, and she liked Ralegh and was relieved that – unlike some of her other favourites, some of whom obviously had ideas of marrying her and becoming King of England – he was just an attractive flirt. They soon became fast friends.

One of the results of being a close friend of a king or queen is that almost everyone else becomes jealous and suspicious of you. Most of the men of Elizabeth's court, who would have loved to call themselves the Queen's friend, were very upset indeed at Ralegh's sudden rise to favour. He quickly became *"the best hated man of the world, in Court, city and country"*. That was said by a courtier who disliked him. It was not true, but Ralegh was certainly not popular.

His unpopularity reached its height when people learned just how rich the Queen was making him: she gave him the right to issue licences to sell wine, and this alone brought him in £1,100 (£264,000 today) a year – more than the income of many noblemen. Then there was a licence to export woollen cloth, one of the country's great exports, which earned another £3,500 a year. Ralegh might not have had Drake's freedom of action, but he was now a very rich man indeed.

Drake
Around the World
1576 – 1580

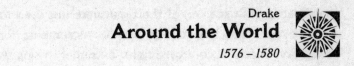

ONE OF DRAKE'S MAIN REASONS for wanting to explore
the Pacific was certainly to upset the Spanish, who so far
had been almost completely alone in making the
dangerous voyage through the Strait of Magellan, which
winds for 600 km between the mainland of South
America and the island of Tierra del Fuego and connects
the South Atlantic to the South Pacific. No one yet
knew that the Pacific could be reached another way, by
the route around Cape Horn at the southernmost point
of Tierra del Fuego, which could be even more
dangerous in bad weather.

It was the Portuguese navigator Fernao de Magalhaes
– who the English usually call Ferdinand Magellan – who
was first to cross the Pacific Ocean and had given it its
name. The Spanish adventurers that followed believed
that the very fact that their ships were sailing in the

Pacific was an argument for their owning any continent they might come across there. Drake disagreed.

One problem he faced when setting out for the Pacific was that English seamen at the time were not used to long voyages and the lack of proper instruments for navigation made such expeditions extremely risky. A ship's longitude (its position east or west of any particular point) could not yet be discovered at sea, and it was very difficult to find its latitude (its position north or south of the equator). This had to be done by standing on the deck of a pitching ship, often in heavy seas, and trying to calculate the exact angle between yourself and the Sun and other heavenly bodies. Not surprisingly, the result was usually very inaccurate, and when ships were successful in reaching their destinations with little delay and without detours, it had much to do with luck and intelligent guesswork. It was almost impossible to discover exactly where you were, in the middle of a vast ocean.

This did not, however, deter the great Elizabethan explorers and Drake knew that there were others as eager as he to earn fame through making new discoveries. His old Plymouth friend John Oxenham, who had stood with him on the high hill in Panama when he had first seen the Pacific, was already planning his own expedition. So was another fine seaman, Richard Grenville. Oxenham, in fact, beat his old commander to the starting-line, and in April 1576 sailed from Plymouth with two ships and 57 men, many of whom had previously travelled with Drake. Oxenham reached the Gulf of Panama, but was taken by the Spanish and eventually executed.

Meanwhile, Drake was raising money for his own expedition and seeking support from anyone who was prepared to help, including a number of courtiers – the Queen's old friend the Earl of Leicester and her Secretary of State Francis Walsingham were among them. Rather like Drake, they were as interested in upsetting Spain as in making a profit.

The official plan was that Drake should sail through the Strait of Magellan and make friends with the natives along the coast of what is now Chile. (He set £50 aside to buy presents for the Indians.) Then he would explore the area thoroughly, and return with what cargo he could find, probably spices. Unofficially, both the Queen and her advisers let it be known that if he came across a Spanish ship or two and robbed them, no one would object. When Drake said goodbye to Elizabeth, she told him: *"I would gladly be revenged on the King of Spain for divers [various] injuries that I have received,"* adding, *"I account that he who striketh thee, Drake, striketh me."*

Despite the Queen's unofficial endorsement she wasn't prepared to lend him a ship, and so he set about building one. It would become perhaps the most famous of all English ships, at first called the *Pelican*, then, later, the *Golden Hind*. She was tiny compared to today's ships

– only 70 feet long – but sturdy, with extra-strong timbers and masts strengthened to carry extra sails, and armed with 18 guns. She was to sail with four even smaller craft, the *Elizabeth*, the *Marigold*, the *Swan* and the *Benedict* – the first two with 16 guns each, the *Swan* with five and the little *Benedict* (only 15 tons) with one.

Below decks were stored gunpowder and shot, muskets, hand weapons including crossbows, suits of armour, and the usual supplies of food: casks of biscuit, beans, peas, lentils, salt, beer, honey, beef, pork, cheese and rice. On the deck were four pinnaces. Harpoons and fishing gear were also taken, so that the crew could fish whenever possible, to increase the supply of fresh food.

Drake himself was going to live in luxury. He might give the impression of a rough sailor, but he liked his comforts. He had acquired a taste for fine clothes, and in his cabin his huge sea-chest contained well-cut, colourful garments, including a fine seaman's cap, a present from the Queen, embroidered with the words *"The Lord guide and preserve thee until the end"*. There were maps, books and instruments of navigation, globes showing the countries of the world and the stars in the skies, the Bible and several other books, with cushions, embroidered rugs and silver plates and dishes. Down in the hold, next to the barrels that held the beer for his crew, were casks of the finest wine and boxes of crystallized fruit and sweets for Drake himself.

It would have been difficult to find any seaman in Plymouth who would have not considered it an honour to sail with Drake, though the 80 men and boys who were packed into the *Pelican*, and the 80 more who sailed in the other ships were nowhere near as comfortable as Drake. Today, if you visit one of the life-size models of ships of the period, it is very difficult to believe that so many men could actually have lived in such a small space. Drake's brother Thomas and his 15-year-old cousin John sailed with him, as did Diego, the black cimarron, as the captain's devoted personal servant.

At last, all was ready. At 5 pm on 15 November 1577 the fleet sailed out of Plymouth Sound. Drake had told his men that they were going for a comfortable cruise in the Mediterranean and they must have been delighted at the thought of spending some of the cold English winter in the warmth of the waters off Italy and Greece. It was, of course, completely untrue. Drake knew that all sailors had heard stories about how dangerous the Strait of Magellan was, and didn't want his men to spend more time than they had to in worrying about whether they were going to get through it safely.

Meanwhile, the Spaniards knew that something was up. *"Francis Drake is going to the Antilles* [the islands of the West Indies]*."* King Philip was told. *"It is important to know the location in order to send them to the bottom of the sea"*. But the Spanish spies were short of real knowledge – they had been fed false information, which they did not believe, but they had no other intelligence.

Like so many of Drake's voyages, this one began badly. Storms forced the ships into Falmouth for protection and even within that wonderfully safe harbour they were so damaged that they had to return to Plymouth for repairs. On 13 December they set out again, and all too soon the crews found themselves not in the Mediterranean but off the coast of north-west Africa. If this worried them, they cheered up when they caught and captured six Spanish and Portuguese ships – one of them carrying fresh food. Drake was especially pleased at taking the *Santa Maria*, for on board was a Portuguese pilot, Nuño da Silva, who was familiar with the sea between Europe and South America, and had several useful maps. Drake persuaded da Silva to accompany them, re-named the *Santa Maria* the *Mary* (perhaps after his wife?) and took it along, putting Thomas Doughty, a small-time investor in the voyage, in charge of her.

Doughty upset the crew right away by pocketing some of the treasure from the hold of the *Mary*. This rightly belonged to the whole crew, and should have been divided up among them. When the men protested, Doughty began trying to get them on his side. He suggested that they might break away from the other ships, desert Drake, and go off to do a little piracy on their own. He made a bad mistake. Drake was more popular with his crew than Doughty could ever be, and the news soon reached the commander that Doughty was planning mutiny. He was keen to avoid trouble that early in the voyage, so he transferred Doughty to the

Pelican. But Doughty continued to tempt the crew to rebel, and Drake was forced to put him on board the *Swan* more or less as a prisoner.

The little fleet reached the coast of Brazil, and sailed south to the shore of what is now Argentina. Doughty, supported by his brother John, was still trying to persuade Drake's men to rebel against their commander, and when they loyally refused, he told Francis Fletcher, the fleet's parson, that he would end any chance of Drake's success by setting man against man until the expedition was uncontrollable. He would make them cut each other's throats, he said. He and his brother also upset the crew of the *Pelican* by claiming that they were wizards, able to raise devils to help them take over the expedition. Seamen were often very superstitious and fearful of anything which might be "magic" and this claim made them afraid of Doughty.

Drake finally lost his temper, hit Doughty, and ordered him to be tied to the mainmast, telling the crew that he and his brother were *"a very bad couple, the which he did not know how to carry along with them"*. Thomas was *"a conjurer, a seditious fellow and a very bad and lewd fellow"* and as for John, *"I cannot tell from whence he came, but from the Devil, I think"*.

Soon the fleet would have to brave the threatening waters of the Magellan Strait. There would probably be very bad weather, and it was absolutely necessary that the crew wasn't distracted by Doughty's troublemaking. It was time for action. All the men were ordered ashore on a sandy island off the coast, and there a trial was held. Drake made a final speech:

> *My masters, consider what a great voyage we are like to make, the like was never made out of England, for by the same the worst in this fleet shall become a gentleman, and if this voyage go not forward, which I cannot see how possibly it should if this man live, what a reproach it will be… Therefore, my masters, they that think this man worthy to die, let them with me hold up their hands.*

There was no hesitation. Doughty was condemned and executed. Drake held up his head, according to custom, with the words *"Lo! This is the end of traitors"*. Doughty's brother was allowed to live. When, eventually, they returned to England he tried to rouse feeling against Drake for the execution; but there was unanimous opinion, not only among seamen, that anyone who attempted mutiny deserved the death penalty.

Drake spoke again to the men of the expedition. His message was a simple one – they must all pull together, seaman and gentleman:

> *We are very far from our country and friends. We are compassed in on every side with our enemies… Wherefore we must have these mutinies and discords that are grown amongst us redressed, for by the life of God it doth even take my wits from me to think on*

it... I must have the gentleman to haul and draw with the mariner, and the mariner with the gentleman. What, let us show ourselves all to be of a company!

Now Drake had to turn to the other problem. He was concerned that the ships of the little fleet should all stay together. Storms often meant separation. The fewer ships there were, the better that chance was. He had already ordered the *Swan* to be broken up, and now decided that the *Mary* must be burned. Only the *Elizabeth*, the *Marigold* and the *Pelican* set sail again. As they sighted the entrance to the Strait of Magellan, and waited for a favourable wind, Drake held a service and re-named the *Pelican* the *Golden Hind* in honour of Christopher Hatton, the Captain of the Queen's Guard (a golden hind, or female deer, was on the coat of arms on Hatton's shield).

The Strait of Magellan was a test for any seaman – there were tales of dreadful snow-storms, mountainous waves and razor-sharp rocks, and most of them were true. Alhough none of the men on board Drake's ships had sailed in those waters before – not even the Portuguese navigator, Nuño da Silva – everybody feared the coming test. Fortunately, the weather was as good as anyone could have hoped, and the fleet sailed safely and quickly through the almost 600-km passage, with great snowy cliffs of rock on either side. They paused only once, at an island where they killed 2,000 penguins for food.

The whole company must have felt relieved as after only 14 days they sailed into the south Pacific. But their relief was short-lived. Drake turned north-west, making for Peru, but almost immediately thick fog and flurries of snow came down, and it very soon became clear that the charts he carried were inaccurate – they should have been sailing due north. Just as he corrected their course, they were hit by a terrible storm. The *Marigold* sank in tumultuous seas, the whole crew drowned.

The *Elizabeth*, separated from the *Golden Hind*, was lucky enough to find a cove where she was protected from the storm. When the winds dropped, the captain, William Winter, *"through a kind of desire that some in her had to be out of these troubles, and to be at home again"*, as he later said, decided to desert Drake. He sailed back through the strait, and reached Plymouth in June 1579 with the news that Drake had reached the Pacific, but that there had been no sign of him after the great storm that had blown them apart; there was little chance he and his crew could still be alive.

In fact, Drake had survived, but the *Golden Hind* was now the only English ship in the vast and unknown waters ahead of him. He had already begun to make important discoveries. He had found, for instance, that the Magellan Strait was not, as everyone had believed, a sea passage between South America and another vast continent, known as Terra Australis Incognita – the unknown southern country. What lay south of Tierra del Fuego was simply another vast stretch of sea. (It was almost 200 years before Captain Cook claimed Australia in the name of the King of England.)

The *Golden Hind* fought the storm for six weeks before the winds gradually weakened. On 28 October Drake was able to anchor at the island of Mocha, just off the coast of Chile. The natives at first seemed friendly, but then suddenly attacked a landing party in huge numbers and wounded every member of it – including Drake himself – with a shower of poisoned arrows. They were in serious trouble, for the ship's surgeon was dead, and though there was another on the *Elizabeth*, she was nowhere to be seen. Drake, with an arrow wound in his face, nursed his men with the help of a cabin boy *"whose goodwill was more than any skill he had"*.

They all recovered. Drake refused to revenge himself on the natives, though he had the guns to do it. He was sure that they had thought his crew were Spaniards, and that the attack had been a mistake. He sailed on, hoping to find the *Marigold* and the *Elizabeth*, but without success.

At Valparaiso, an important seaport of Chile on the west coast of south America, Drake broke into some Spanish storehouses, taking food and some gold ornaments. In December, he put into the port of Santiago, 60 miles to the west-north-west of Valparaiso, and easily captured a Spanish ship that lay at anchor, before going ashore and looting the town of gold, silver and casks of wine.

Single-handedly, Drake was making war on the whole of Chile and Peru. He would not have been able to fight all the Spanish ships in the area if they had come at him at once, but he could sail quietly among them, attacking one here and another there. It was not always easy, though. On 19 December he put a party ashore on an island to collect fresh water, but a party of Spaniards suddenly appeared and shot one of his men before they could retreat. The English watched as the Spanish cut off the man's head, and tore out his heart – another example of the cruelty that made them so hated.

There were disappointments, too, when captured ships and the towns they attacked turned out to have no treasure. The Spanish now knew that "El Draque" was among them, and were taking special care to keep their gold and silver out of his way.

But there was one special and magnificent prize: the *Nuestra Señora de la Concepción*, a huge galleon that was on her way back to Spain and was said to carry treasure. (Not all Spanish ships were "galleons". In fact, when Drake first fought them, they were small three-masted ships. Because of his success in capturing so many of them, the Spanish built larger ones, with three decks from which cannon could be fired, but they were never so easy to sail as the English ships Drake commanded.)

Drake offered a gold chain to the first man to spot the *Nuestra Señora*. She was eventually sighted at Cabo de San Francisco, four miles off the Peruvian coast.

Drake slowed the *Golden Hind* down by trailing mattresses and ropes behind her, so as not to catch up with his prey too quickly and give her the opportunity to hoist more sail and get away. He sneaked up on her as darkness was falling, and brought down one of her masts with a single shot. She had no guns, and surrendered immediately. Fourteen chests of silver coins, 80 pounds of gold and 26 tons of silver – more than Drake could possibly have hoped for – were carried onto the *Golden Hind* while the unfortunate Spanish commander stood watching helplessly. He was released afterwards and allowed to sail home with his much-lighter craft.

Drake behaved politely to Captain Ana and his crew, even giving them some of their own goods back so that they would not go home without any money or clothes at all. He offered one man a mirror to take home to his wife, gave some of the crew a few small guns and swords, so that they would not be defenceless, and bestowed on Ana, as the Spaniard later reported:

> *...a basin of gilded silver with a name written in the middle of it which said "Francisqus Draques", and at the same time he turned me loose he gave me a safe conduct [a letter] in English signed with his name, telling me that he gave it to me so that if the other two English ships which had been reported to be behind him should fall in with [come across] me they would not do me any harm or rob me again.*

Drake went on to take several more prizes. The greatest was a ship from Acapulco in Mexico, commanded by its owner, Don Francisco de Carate, who in a letter to the Spanish Viceroy wrote excitedly about "El Draque":

He is about thirty-five years old, of small size, with a reddish beard, and is one of the greatest sailors that exist, both from his skill and from his power of commanding. His ship is of near four hundred tons, sails well, and has a hundred men, all in the prime of life and as well trained for war as if they were old soldiers of Italy. Each one is especially careful to keep his arms [weapons] clean. He treats them with affection, and they him with respect. He has with him nine or ten gentlemen, younger sons of the leading men in England, who form his council; he calls them together on every occasion and hears what they have to say, but he is not bound by their advice, though he may be guided by it. He has no privacy; these of whom I speak all dine at his table... The service is of silver, richly gilt, and engraved with his arms; he has too all possible luxuries, even to perfumes, many of which he told me were given him by the Queen. None of these gentlemen sits down or puts on his hat in his presence without repeated permission. He dines and sups to the music of violins.

His ship carries thirty large guns, and a great quantity of all sorts of ammunition, as well as artificers [workmen] who can execute necessary repairs. He has two draughtsmen [artists] who portray the coast in its own colours, a thing which troubled me much to see, because everything is put so naturally that any one following him, will have no difficulty.

With his ship low in the water because of the weight of the treasure he had taken, it was time for Drake to make for home. But which way should he go? He did not fancy the Strait of Magellan again – he might not be so lucky next time. He had learned of the route around Cape Horn from the Spanish, but no one knew much about it, and it sounded dangerous. He could sail further north and try to find the north-west passage, which was believed to pass from the north Pacific to the Atlantic. Or – the most exciting possibility – he could sail on westward to the East Indies and complete a journey right around the world, something which many people still believed to be impossible.

At first, he preferred the idea of the north-west passage, and sailed in that direction. But as the ship got further and further north, it got colder and colder, and when the ropes and rigging froze he changed his mind and turned south again, then west, to sail right across the Pacific. He and his crew spent 68 anxious days at sea without sight of land. No radio, remember, to keep in touch with home or talk to friends. They must have felt more isolated, more alone, than man has ever felt in space. Then they came across a little island – no one is quite sure which – where they thought they could land to find some fresh water and possibly some food. But the natives, after taking gifts from them, attacked them so violently that Drake was forced to open fire, killing several of them.

On he sailed, past the Philippines and on to the Moluccas, the Indonesian "spice islands", where he landed on the island of Ternate. The Portuguese had reached the islands some years earlier, and had taken home many rich cargoes of spices. Drake thought that perhaps an English ship would not be welcome, but fortunately Baber, the Sultan of Ternate, was at war with the Portuguese, who had killed his father. He was delighted to welcome Drake as a possible ally.

Three splendid galleys towed the *Golden Hind* to a safe anchorage, and Baber himself came to welcome Drake, dressed in all his finery: a cloth-of-gold belt around his waist, enormous quantities of gold and diamond jewellery on his hands and around his neck, and red leather shoes. Drake gave him a splendid velvet cloak and also seems to have given him some sort of promise to help expel the Portuguese from the island. (A treaty against the Portuguese was imposed, but never formally signed.) Drake loaded six tons of cloves – a valuable cargo – and after repairing his ship and taking on fresh water sailed on westwards into waters for which no maps existed.

Sailing in and out of small islands off the coast of Celebes, east of Borneo, Drake was constantly worried that he might strike an area where the water wasn't deep enough to take his ship – and rightly so, for on 9 January 1580 the *Golden Hind* ran onto rocks just beneath the water. Drake had to get her off quickly, before a rough sea could rock her to and fro on the reef so roughly that her timbers would crack. He threw three tons of cloves overboard, together with two cannon and various supplies but the ship was still aground. Then, suddenly, a gust of wind lifted her and swung her off the reef and into deep water.

The damage was not as bad as Drake had feared, and he was able to sail on and arrive safely at Java, where he took on food and water to keep his crew alive and healthy on the almost two-month voyage to the coast of Africa and the Cape of Good Hope. He sailed easily around the Cape – the weather was very calm – but by the time he reached Sierra Leone the water casks were almost empty, and despite collecting rain-water the crew was given a daily ration of less than half a pint for every three men.

At Sierra Leone water and fresh fruit were taken aboard, and when the crew went ashore they enjoyed the surprising sight of a monstrous grey creature, which the locals called an elephant. Then on they went, on the last stretch for home. On 26 September 1580, fishermen in the English Channel saw a small ship making for Plymouth. As they passed, a crewman shouted, *"The Queen – does she still live?"* She did; and Drake and his men landed again on her England.

Elizabeth had heard news – or rather exaggerated tales – of Drake from time to time, but it was impossible to tell what might be true and what was perhaps just a rumour. Had he actually executed one of his men? Could the Spanish be telling the truth when they claimed that he was sailing all over the West Indies, doing deeds of piracy as daring as those of earlier years? Complaint after complaint reached London from the King of Spain, but Bernardino de Mendoza, the Spanish Ambassador in London, wasn't able to tell Philip that the Queen – or anyone else – was sorry for the confusion "El Draque" was causing. *"The adventurers who provided money and ships for Drake's voyage are beside themselves for joy"* he wrote, *"and the people here are talking of nothing else but going out to plunder in a similar way."*

In Plymouth Sound, the great seaman stayed on his little ship for a while. There was plague in the town, and he didn't want to catch it, though he welcomed his wife on board, together with the Mayor. As soon as news of his arrival reached London he was told to report there, bringing some souvenirs of his journey, by which Drake knew the Queen meant treasure. He loaded up some gold and silver and rode to the capital, leaving the *Golden Hind* for the time being at anchor in Plymouth.

He was alone with the Queen for over six hours, telling her of his adventures. She was to summon him again and again and never tired of hearing his tales. When he left her, it was with orders that all the treasure he had brought back should be brought to the Tower of

London for safekeeping – except £10,000-worth, which he could keep for himself. By making sure everyone heard this, the Queen ensured that any complaints the Spanish made about stolen gold and silver could never be satisfied, because nobody would know just how much there was. It is likely that Drake took more than his allotted £10,000 of treasure, and he certainly took a substantial amount in addition to this to share amongst his crew. It is said that privately he gave the Queen treasure to the value of £100,000 before taking what remained – perhaps as much as £264,000 – to the Tower.

Whatever the total sum was, it was astonishing – possibly as much as £600,000 (almost one and a half billion punds today) – and the Queen's expenses for a whole year amounted to only £250,000. The Spanish Ambassador was hopping mad, and getting no real information out of anyone. Elizabeth assured him that Drake had done no damage at all to Spain and that if this was found to be untrue, she would personally see that the King was repaid. Mendoza had no way of discovering how much Spanish treasure Drake had taken, and Drake cheekily told him that if any had been found to be missing, it had probably been stolen by the Spanish crews themselves.

All this argument about money did not stop anyone from being amazed and impressed by Drake's extraordinary round-the-world journey. He was the man of the moment, and for the first time the centre of attention at court. If Ralegh was able to delight the

Queen with poetry and sweet conversation, Drake could tell wonderful stories of the most remarkable journey of the century. The Queen was delighted by his company – one day she sent for him no fewer than nine times – and if her other favourites grumbled that he was an uneducated provincial upstart, she retorted angrily that she enjoyed his stories, bluffly told in that thick Devonshire accent.

Drake took pleasure in throwing his new-found money around. Mendoza, infuriated, complained to King Philip that he was:

> ...*squandering more money than any man in England... He gave to the Queen a crown [which] she wore on New Year's Day. It has in it five emeralds, three of them almost as long as a middle finger, whilst the two round ones are valued at 20,000 crowns, coming as they do from Peru. He has also given the Queen a diamond cross as a New Year's gift, as is the custom here, of the value of 5,000 crowns.*
>
> *The Queen shows extraordinary favour to Drake, and never fails to speak to him when she goes out in public, conversing with him for a long time. She says that she will knight him on the day she goes to see his ship. She has ordered the ship itself to be brought ashore and placed in her arsenal near Greenwich as a curiosity.*

And so it was; and so she did.

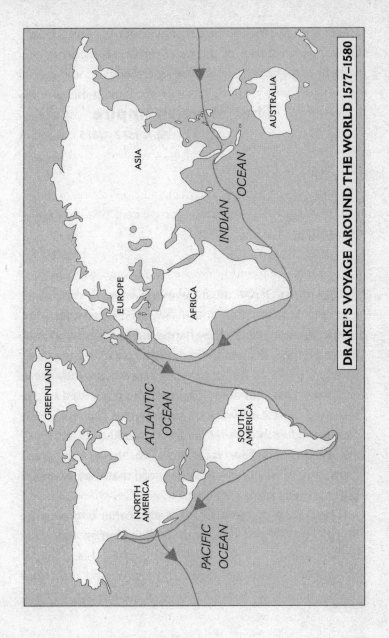

DRAKE'S VOYAGE AROUND THE WORLD 1577–1580

AUSTRALIA

ASIA

INDIAN OCEAN

EUROPE

AFRICA

GREENLAND

ATLANTIC OCEAN

SOUTH AMERICA

NORTH AMERICA

PACIFIC OCEAN

The "Brytish Impire"
Early 1582 – 1585

RALEGH AND DRAKE must have known each other, and met – or at least been in the same room together – on many occasions when they happened to be in London at the same time. Both of them needed to show themselves to the Queen, to make sure she knew who they were and what they had done. She was the royal road to the top. And her Court was not so large that two such men could avoid each other even if they wanted to. Yet there are surprisingly few references to these two great Elizabethans meeting – and no record that they swapped tales or made plans together.

They may have disliked each other's company. Ralegh, the elegant poet with his fine clothes and witty conversation, may have thought his fellow Westcountryman uncivilized and crude, and may have been jealous of his successes on the Spanish Main. Drake

was far less concerned about his personal appearance –
he may have thought of Ralegh as a bit of a snob whose
only sea adventure had ended in disaster. And though he
had no education, he probably had as many books in his
cabin as Ralegh.

Drake was a hands-on seaman, whose attempts to
find a way to the Queen's favour rested on what he
actually did and would do in future: he would bring her
treasure, he would impress her by his courage and risky
adventures. Ralegh may well have wanted to do the
same, but he had become such a close friend of the
Queen that she could not do without him and would not
grant permission for him to go to sea again.

Sir Humphrey Gilbert had set out a year earlier on
another expedition to the New World, as the English
called the unexplored areas of North and South
America. We do not know when Ralegh began to buy, or
even to build, his own ships – but he certainly had more
than one by this time. He had not only given Gilbert
£2,000 towards the expense of the voyage, but had also
lent him a ship, the *Bark Ralegh*, a well-built, fast, heavily
armed vessel. Unfortunately a severe storm struck
almost as soon as Gilbert's fleet left the English coast,
and the *Bark Ralegh* had to turn back. When Gilbert did
manage to cross the Atlantic his largest remaining vessel
was wrecked with the loss of 84 men. Gilbert and his
crew got on to the smallest surviving ship, the little

Squirrel. His crew attempted to persuade him to sail in a larger ship. If they were hit by another storm, they said, the *Squirrel* would be the first to sink. But he refused. Another storm did strike, and Gilbert was drowned, last seen sitting in the stern reading a book as the mountainous waves overcame the ship. (*"We are as near to heaven by sea as by land,"* he told his crew.)

When he heard of the tragedy Ralegh felt he must carry on Gilbert's work. In the spring of 1584 he planned a voyage that would not only impress the Queen, but claim new lands in her name. He persuaded her to order him to:

> ...*discover, search, find out and view such remote, to heathen and barbarous lands, countries and territories, not actually possessed by any Christian prince, not inhabited by Christian people.*

She had granted the same licence to his half-brother, but this time what he had in mind was the stealing not of treasure, but of land. He thought (and the Queen agreed) that an educated European had a perfect right to take over land occupied only by natives who could not read or write.

He asked the clergyman and writer Richard Hakluyt to help him prepare an advertisement announcing a new voyage. He wanted to convince the rich and powerful that there was good land to be found in the New World, and therefore good money. If a settlement was set up to the west of the Atlantic, settlers – including *"numbers of idle men"*, by which he meant convicts – could produce wine, olive oil and silk, and send this home together with gold and silver, copper and pearls.

To help persuade people to put money into the plan, Ralegh went to John Dee, a scientist, scholar, philosopher and astrologer (he had advised the Queen of the precise moment when the planets said she should be crowned). Dee was a man after Ralegh's own heart: he argued that England should challenge Spain's claim to the New World. Years earlier Pope Alexander VI had issued a Bull – a special order – dividing these new lands between Spain and Portugal, with Portugal controlling the routes to the West Indies, and Spain having the right to any discoveries made in North and South America west of Brazil. Now, because Spain had hundreds of colonies in America, and for years had been bringing back to Europe enormous quantities of gold and silver, it was generally accepted that the country was entitled to rule the whole area. Dee thought this was nonsense, and so did Ralegh.

Ten years earlier, Dee had told the Queen that she should take the title of Empress, and increase her navy by at least 50 large ships (she then had only 34 warships, while Spain had over 200). He believed that she could reign over a *"Brytish Impire"* – the first known mention of a "British Empire"), which would challenge and defeat all those who threatened its domination. It was a claim that both Drake and Ralegh favoured, although it was a very brave idea. England, after all, was a small island nation, while Spain had a great empire and huge riches.

Dee believed that control of the seas and the setting up of British colonies abroad was the best way of challenging Spain. He thought that the Queen had rights over most of the seas and many of the lands in the northern half of the world. The Queen was so impressed by his ideas that she called on him at his house at Mortlake, taking Ralegh with her to hear more of them. (Drake, incidentally, also knew Dee and relied on his advice on maps and navigation.)

Drake and other pirates had forced Spain to guard her treasure ships more closely, and there were no longer such rich pickings to be found on the Spanish Main. The idea of settlements that would actually produce spices, hides and other things to send home was an excellent one. What is more, such settlements would provide useful harbours from which English pirates could slip down the coast and attack the Spanish with lively crews not exhausted after a tiring Atlantic crossing. King Philip would soon find *"his old bands of soldiers dissolved, his purpose defeated, his powers and strength diminished, his pride abated, and his tyranny utterly suppressed"*, as Dr Dee put it. His armies would be disbanded, his pride broken and control of his great empire ended. It was a very good idea indeed.

Dee had met the great European map-makers and navigators, and had brought back from Europe a "cross-staff", a new and more accurate means of measuring the height of the stars and therefore more easily discovering position at sea. At Durham House, where Ralegh lived in handsome apartments given to him by the Queen, he showed off a huge map of the North American coastline from Canada down to Florida and Mexico. He also befriended Thomas Hariot, a mathematician who taught navigation to Philip Amadas and Arthur Barlow, two Plymouthians who were later to captain Ralegh's ships.

Ralegh examined Dee's map carefully, and found a bay between the West Indies and Newfoundland which looked like an excellent place at which to set up a colony. He sent two ships to produce more detailed maps of the Bahia de Santa Maria, or St Mary's Bay. They sailed in April 1584, and sent back an enthusiastic report about the place. Rows of peas grew over a foot high within ten days, they said, and other vegetables and grapes grew equally well. There was plenty of fish and wild animals to be caught for food, and it seemed likely that there was gold and silver to be mined. The ships returned with the good news, and with two Indians who had agreed to travel to England to help produce a dictionary of the local language. Ralegh found some clothes for them, and they were presented to the Queen, "properly" dressed instead of wearing the few skins that were their usual attire.

Elizabeth was pleased to accept Ralegh's suggestion that when the colony was established, it should be known, in her honour, as "Virginia" (she was known as "the Virgin Queen"). She was so delighted by the proposal that she made him a knight. The honour did not please his rivals at court. Being the favourite of the Queen made a lot of people jealous, especially the handsome 17-year-old 2nd Earl of Essex (Robert Devereux), who was well on his way to becoming Ralegh's main rival for the Queen's favour. There was going to be trouble with him: he was very eager to become a close friend to the Queen, and hated the fact that Ralegh was so close to her. *"That knave Ralegh"*, he called him, and would often be extremely rude about him, even in his hearing – something Ralegh only put up with because he could not fight in Elizabeth's presence.

Almost all Ralegh's money was tied up in planning the colony of Virginia, and the expenses were great. He longed to go along with the expedition. Drake, in his place, would have been off like a shot, and the Queen would not have stopped him. But whatever he said, she firmly refused permission for Ralegh to leave the country. Lonely, as kings and queens often are, she simply didn't want to lose him. He was always surprising and pleasing her with his words and actions. Most men were much too afraid of a Queen whose whims could change at a moment's notice to tease her or make a joke with her. Ralegh wasn't afraid and she loved it.

She was careful to praise Ralegh for his part in the new project, naming him in Latin, *Domini et Gubernatoria Virginiae* – Lord and Governor of Virginia. She also lent

Sir Francis Drake stands with his hand on a globe of the world (in reference to his voyage around it). He wears a necklace given to him by the Queen, which contained her portrait.

Walter Ralegh dressed for the court of Queen Elizabeth. She kept him at her side when he would rather have been fighting the Spaniards.

ÆTATIS SVÆ LViii
1591

Francis Drake's relative, Sir John Hawkins, was the first Englishman to
buy and sell slaves. He also organized the fleet against the Spanish Armada
and bravely sailed with it.

*Sir Walter Ralegh planned the first English colony in North America; the
English flag was set up in Virginia in 1586.*

The story that Sir Walter Ralegh laid down his cloak over a puddle to protect the Queen's shoes is just a tale; but it was the kind of action he might have taken as a friend to the Queen.

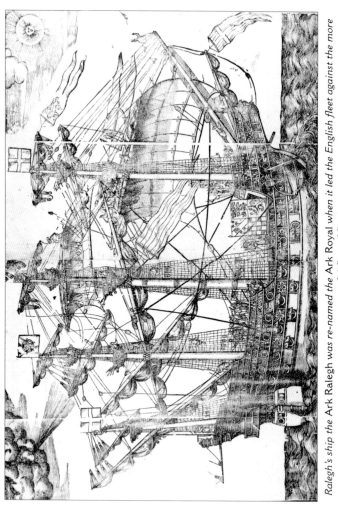

Ralegh's ship the Ark Ralegh was re-named the Ark Royal when it led the English fleet against the more powerful fleet of Spain.

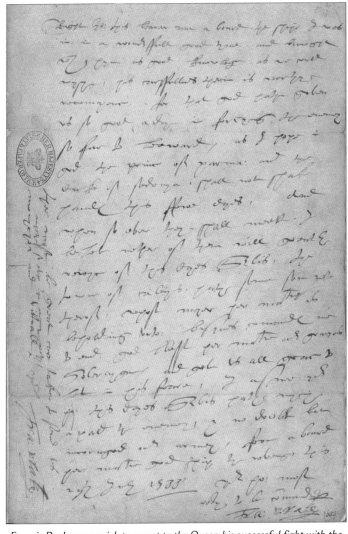

Francis Drake was quick to report to the Queen his successful fight with the ships of the Spanish Armada. This letter was written during the battle and sent to Elizabeth's private secretary, Sir Francis Walsingham.

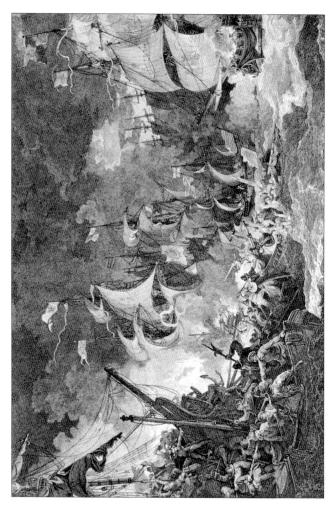

No artist was present at the defeat of the Spanish Armada – but many have since given, in imaginary pictures like this, their idea of what the great battle might have looked like.

him a ship to send on the expedition to St Mary's Bay, the *Tyger*, into which he put his cousin Sir Richard Grenville as captain. Grenville had always been jealous of Drake; now he was delighted to command the new venture. How Ralegh must have envied him!

The fleet sailed on 9 April 1585. Spanish spies, keeping their eyes on the scheming English (it was only a matter of months before England and Spain were at war) counted 16 ships which they thought held over 400 men. In fact there were only eight ships, but over 800 men crowded into them. Grenville paused on the way to capture four Spanish vessels and seize their cargoes. Any treasure he could get hold of would help to pay for the venture, and in any case it was good fun. But within sight of the Bahia de Santa Maria, he had a stroke of bad luck and ran the *Tyger* ashore on a sandbank. Her hold was flooded and a large part of the expedition's provisions were spoiled.

However, Grenville, Hariot and Amadas conducted a thorough survey of the whole area, and though the land turned out at first to be not as good as they had been led to believe, some miles up the coast a local Indian chief showed them the island of Roanoke, fertile, with plenty of water, and in a good position for defence. In August 1585, the chief offered them the island and 108 settlers immediately set about building a small village in which they could spend the coming winter. Ralph Lane, a wealthy young courtier the Queen had named as the Governor of any new colony, was left in control, and

Grenville returned to give Ralegh the news that the first English colony had been established in the New World. The area became, years later, one of the original 13 states of the USA, and thanks to Ralegh is still named in honour of the great English Queen.

On the way home, Grenville met a large Spanish trading ship and took her cargo of ginger and sugar, worth £50,000. When Ralegh heard of his arrival at Plymouth, he hurried down with a number of people who had put money into the voyage, to meet and congratulate him. When she heard the good news, the Queen gave Ralegh the credit and several more positions which, not especially important on their own, brought him a lot of money. He became Master of Horse, Lord Warden of the Stannaries (which gave him control of the tin industry) and Lord Lieutenant of Cornwall (which gave him control of the Cornish coast). He was also made Captain of the Queen's Guard, and was granted several pieces of valuable land – he owned three manors in Lincolnshire, a manor in Derbyshire, and lands in Nottinghamshire. Drake, by comparison, was still poor.

Drake
Sir Francis
1581 – 1585

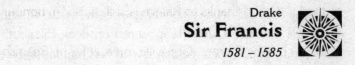

ON 1 APRIL 1581 Queen Elizabeth travelled down the Thames to Deptford, where the *Golden Hind* lay out of the water, in dry dock. News had got around that this would be the day that she would pay tribute to Drake, and thousands of people turned out to watch her being rowed down the river in her state barge, and her arrival at the dock. There, she crossed a wooden bridge onto the deck of the little vessel. She was followed by so many people that the bridge collapsed, catapulting a number of Londoners into the Thames mud.

Drake, magnificently dressed, welcomed his Queen on board. She was clearly in a very good mood. When one of her purple-and-gold garters came loose and slid down her leg, trailing behind her on one foot, and the French Ambassador gallantly picked it up, she wasn't at all embarrassed, but just put her foot up on a rail and replaced the garter, telling M. de Marchaumont that she would send it to him as a gift when she had finished with it.

Drake had laid on a splendid banquet in his cabin, and when he and the Queen reappeared on deck Elizabeth told him to kneel, and a golden sword was handed to her. It would be just the moment, she joked, to cut off his head as the King of Spain had asked (not a very funny joke from someone who could easily order your execution). Instead she handed the sword to M. de Marchaumont and gave him the power to make Drake a knight. This was a clever move, because what she was doing was ordering the Ambassador to do something that would publicly honour the great enemy of Spain, and might be thought to suggest that France was on England's side. However, he made the gesture, and Sir Francis Drake rose to his feet.

It was the proudest moment of his life. A knighthood was a real honour. The *Golden Hind* was also honoured: the Queen instructed that she should be preserved for all time. A wall was built around the dock, and the ship lay there for many years, visited by thousands of people. (Unfortunately, little or nothing was known about how to preserve her, and what with dry rot and the visitors' habit of breaking pieces off her to take home as souvenirs, virtually nothing was left of the great little ship by the end of the seventeenth century.)

Among the crowd at Deptford on that April day was one man who didn't do any cheering – John Doughty, the brother of the executed rebel. The Queen, he told anyone who would listen, had honoured *"the arrantest knave, the vilest villain, the falsest thief and the cruellest murderer that ever was born"*. Someone who overheard him reported him to the Privy Council, and Doughty was arrested and thrown into prison, never to be heard of again.

Drake was now the most famous and popular man in England. Portraits of him were painted, copied and passed around, and people told each other again and again the story of his extraordinary journey – a three-year voyage of not far off 40,000 miles, during which Drake had cared for his crew, managing to find fresh food and clean water. And, as one writer put it after his death, he had been:

> *...more skilful in all points of navigation than any that ever was before his time, in his time, or since his death. He was also of perfect memory, great observation, eloquent by nature, skilful in artillery, expert and apt to let blood and give physic [medicine] unto his people.*

Drake was certainly due some peace and quiet for a year or two, so he went down to Devon and bought Buckland Abbey, a thirteenth-century abbey not far from Plymouth. It belonged to the Grenville family, and had been turned into a private house with a fine hall, a handsome drawing-room and bedrooms, and there were some pleasant – although not too large – grounds. Drake bought it for £3,400, and settled in with his wife. It was still his home at the time of his death, although he kept two other houses in Plymouth, which he leased to friends.

The Queen was very generous to him, giving him several estates as well as presents of jewellery, silver and rich clothing. He bought several manors in Devonshire, and 40 houses in Plymouth itself worth over £1,500, including inns and shops. He was an extremely clever businessman, but a generous and caring landlord. The people of Plymouth already admired him as a hero, thought him a great seaman, and loved him as a man. In September 1582 they elected him Mayor, and he took the honour very seriously, interesting himself in local affairs and regularly taking the chair at council meetings where 12 aldermen and 24 councillors discussed local affairs. Over the next few years, he spent much of his time in Plymouth – although in 1584 he entered Parliament, and became a member of various committees dealing with naval affairs.

Drake was also, for the first time in many years, able to spend time at home with his wife Mary. Sadly, she died in 1583. She seems to have been at heart a simple country woman, probably rather overcome at becoming "Lady Drake", but they were clearly happy together though she gave him no children. Drake liked children, and would have liked a son. In old age, Robert Hayman remembered how he had met Drake as a small boy in the street in Totnes, and wrote some verses about it:

A fair red orange in his hand he had.
He gave it me, whereof I was right glad.
Takes and kissed me and prays,
'God bless my boy!'
Which I recall in comfort to this day.

Drake also made or tried to make plans for piracy – there were still Spanish ships loaded with treasure for him to steal; but for one reason and another they all fell through. In 1585 he was married for the second time to a Miss Elizabeth Sydenham, who was more than 20 years younger than he, and the beautiful daughter of the Sheriff of Somerset, a very rich man. Sir Francis and his wife settled at Buckland Abbey, but Drake longed to be back in action against the Spanish. Apart from the riches stored in the holds of their ships, which he would love to get his hands on (he might be a knight, but he was still a pirate at heart), they were now a real danger to England. Soon, he felt sure, the two countries would be at war, and the one who struck the first blow would have the advantage.

Tobacco and Potatoes

1585 – 1587

RALEGH MIGHT NOT have been the great seaman and navigator Drake was – the Queen simply would not let him go to sea, so he had no chance of learning those skills – but he was a very successful pirate, even if he wasn't out on the deck of his ships directing a fight.

Down in the Westcountry, he kept his own private warship, the *Bark Ralegh*, armed and ready not just to go off and attack the Spanish, but to help keep rival pirates in order. His other ships were placed under captains he could trust and sent out on their own piratical expeditions, returning to Plymouth laden with stolen cargoes. The *Bark Randall*, the *Pilgrim* and the *Bark Burton* all brought home rich cargoes of gold, silver, ivory, cloves, hides, sugar, as well as such profitable cargoes as fish, corn, barley and tallow (fat melted down for making candles).

One ship could easily bring back stolen goods worth over £10,000. And it was not only Spain that suffered. Ralegh's ships attacked Italian vessels, too, again with cargoes of spices, as well as rubies, diamonds and pearls. The Italians complained and Ralegh was scolded by the Queen; but alas the cargo in question had been sold within a day or two of being landed at Plymouth, and there was nothing she could do to recover it.

All this piracy was perfectly well known to everyone, even to the Queen, who was careful not to acknowledge it in public, but in private was delighted at any trouble Ralegh and his captains could make for Spain. Charles Howard, Earl of Nottingham and Ralegh's boss, invested money in piracy – and he was the Lord Admiral of England, the Chief Officer of the Navy, and a member of the Queen's Privy Council. What Ralegh and Drake were doing was illegal, but perfectly all right as long as nobody actually talked about it.

During the winter of 1585–86 Drake and Ralegh worked together when Ralegh invested in a fleet organized by his rival to carry out raids on Spain's ports in America. The Queen was also an investor – she contributed £20,000 of the £60,000 (nearly fourteen and a half million pounds today) that it cost to prepare 29 ships and crew them not only with seamen but with 2,300 soldiers. The expedition fell on the Spanish ports like a storm, capturing ships and selling them back to the Spaniards for ready money, as well as taking treasure.

In May 1586, while Drake was sailing round the Caribbean, he did Ralegh a favour by going up the coast of Florida to the port of St Augustine, which Ralegh thought of as a threat to his colony at Roanoke. Drake flattened the town's defences and chased the Spaniards inland, then sailed on to Roanoke itself with supplies for the settlers who had just completed their first year in North America. Another supply ship sent by Ralegh had not yet turned up.

The settlers had endured a difficult year. They couldn't produce enough food for themselves, and the local Indians, though friendly at first, were unable to provide enough food for over 100 hungry Europeans. Believing the natives were as simple-minded as babies, the settlers gave them glass beads, bits of mirror, broken pieces of pottery and wooden toys in exchange. But the Indians, at first attracted by such unusual bits and pieces from Europe, soon realized that they were good for nothing. The settlers also earned a reputation for being magicians or worse. They had brought measles and chickenpox with them, and many defenceless natives died after catching them; because they had no idea how disease was spread, they assumed that the settlers were bewitching them. Thomas Hariot didn't help by doing silly tricks such as starting a fire with a magnifying glass, and showing off a powerful magnet he had brought with him. The natives thought this was clearly bad magic.

The local chief, Wingina, waited until the Governor, Ralph Lane, had led a party far inland looking for gold, then tried to persuade his people to attack and kill the leaders of the settlers. Lane, however, learned of the plan, confronted Wingina, and in a sudden fight killed him and many of his tribe. A week later the sails of Drake's fleet were seen on the horizon.

Drake gave the settlers one of the smaller boats, the *Francis*, to carry them up the coast to another settlement at Chesapeake Bay, but once they were on board, some of the settlers persuaded the crew to sail for home. They had had enough of building the English Empire. Governor Lane was not much more enthusiastic than the deserters. He had no means of knowing whether more supplies were on their way, and he held a meeting of all the citizens of Virginia, who voted unanimously to ask Drake to carry them back to England. On 18 June 1586 they all sailed for Plymouth.

Two days later, Ralegh's supply ship reached Roanoke and found it deserted. It turned back, and on its way to England passed a fleet led by Sir Richard Grenville, which also found Roanoke empty. Grenville left a dozen men to guard the dilapidated settlement, and himself turned for home, engaging in enough piracy on the way to be able to arrive in Devon with no fewer than six prize ships, including a large Spanish galleon laden with spices.

Although Grenville's successful piracy meant that Ralegh hadn't actually lost any money, he wasn't best pleased by Ralph Lane's return. He began a campaign to find new settlers, offering any man who volunteered 500 acres of prime land in Virginia and promising that this time the settlement would really work. Women and children would go, as well as men, he said, and real families would make a real town, properly run and governed. Thomas Hariot produced a book about Virginia – *A Brief and True Report of the New Found Land* – leaving out all the problems and describing the Indians as harmless and good-humoured natives.

He went on to explain that there were all sorts of things that the settlers could grow and prepare there which could be exported back to England, and would make money for the colony: such things as cedar wood, turpentine and tar and sassafras (the leaves of a tree, used to make perfume), which are still produced in the region. And, of course, there was tobacco. Hariot went into raptures about this new drug – it was *"of so precious estimation amongst the Indians that they think their gods are marvellously delighted therewith"*. It brought not just pleasure, but good health, or so they thought.

The smoke from Ralegh's clay pipe was soon polluting the air of the Queen's Court. There is a story that one of his servants, seeing him smoke for the first time, thought his master was on fire and threw a bucket of water over him. He told the Queen (who never seems to have tried tobacco) that he could weigh the smoke and prove that it weighed so little it couldn't possibly do any harm. When she said she thought that was impossible, he carefully weighed the tobacco which went into his pipe, smoked it, then weighed the ashes, and claimed that the difference must represent the smoke. Elizabeth was amused; and she also admired her courtier for the way in which, she said, while others were turning gold into smoke, he was turning smoke into gold. He and others certainly made money from the importing of tobacco, which became so popular that European travellers accused English courtiers of "smoking themselves silly".

Ralegh was not, in fact, the first man to bring tobacco to England – that had been done 20 years earlier by Sir John Hawkins; but Ralegh's name is always associated with it, just as it is also always associated with the potato, which had been introduced into Italy and Spain some time earlier. Ralegh was almost certainly the first man to bring the potato to England, though we must remember, of course, that he did not physically bring either of them, since Elizabeth kept him firmly at home. But he was undoubtedly responsible for their arrival in England.

In 1586, Ralegh had another great success as a pirate. He sent two small ships to the Azores, where they attacked a number of Spanish vessels, and on one of them found Don Pedro Sarmiento de Gamboa, Governor of various Spanish towns around the Strait of Magellan. Although Sarmiento was an enemy, Ralegh was delighted. He welcomed Sarmiento to Plymouth, made sure he was comfortable, and had several enjoyable chats with him. He was specially interested by the Spaniard's stories of a mysterious "golden city" in South America called El Dorado, where untold riches were to be found. An expedition to find this place would really be worthwhile, he thought. More immediately, however, he realized it should be possible to persuade the King of Spain to pay a high ransom for an official like his guest. On reflection, though, he decided it would be worth trying to play a more complicated game. Ralegh had a talk with Sarmiento and made a surprising suggestion. He would let the Spaniard go, provided he went to King Philip and gave him a message that Ralegh had a couple of ships he would be glad to sell him. He was to tell the King that Ralegh really needed the money, and that in future he would be pleased to look out for his interests in England.

It seems an odd business, but it wasn't unusual for Englishmen to sell arms to Spain, and Ralegh made sure the Queen knew of his plans. She was always eager to make money, and knew that he shared her enthusiasm. He introduced Sarmiento to her, and she promised him that if Philip gave orders that his men should stop interfering with English ships, she would keep the English pirates under control. When Sarmiento returned to Spain with the message, however, King Philip was not fooled. He wrote to the Spanish Ambassador in England warning him that Ralegh was not to be trusted.

The Queen probably found the whole situation amusing. Ralegh was still at the centre of her court, one of her most faithful and loving courtiers. He was as close to her, as intimate with her, as any man. He still flirted with her, though he was always careful to make it clear that it was in fun – he had no desire to marry her and become King of England. He kept in touch with scientific advances and modern thought (he had many intelligent friends), and delighted the Queen by writing clever poems to her. One, for instance, consisted of 12 verses, the lines of which could be read either across or downward:

Her face,	Her tongue,	Her wit,
So fair,	So sweet,	So sharp,
First bent,	Then drew,	Then hit,
Mine eye,	Mine ear,	Mine heart...

In 1587 she made him Captain of her Guard, which meant that he was with her almost all the time, from the moment she was dressed in the morning until the moment she went to bed. But it was at this time that the young Earl of Essex came fully into the picture. He was not yet 20, but was very handsome, and as Master of the Queen's Horse, a real rival for Elizabeth's attention and influence. He and Ralegh were always bickering, and sometimes she seemed to favour the younger man, but in the end, Ralegh was the firmer favourite. She actually trusted him. Essex was certainly too young to have earned her faith and she trusted very few of her courtiers.

The Queen showed her favour towards Ralegh in several ways. He was most pleased, though when she put him in charge of a group of men from his own part of England – Devon and Cornwall – who would re-settle parts of Ireland, in particular Munster, which he had got to know well years ago. The idea was that he should take over large parts of the country and persuade English tradespeople and workmen and women – blacksmiths, shopkeepers, farmers and so on – to settle there with their wives and children. They would live ordinary lives, just as they lived in England, and within a short time the Irish (who were thought to be rough and rude and lazy) would almost disappear – southern Ireland would become just like any other English county.

Forty two thousand acres of Munster were "given" to Ralegh and two of his Westcountry friends, Sir John Clifton and Sir John Stowell. The latter two went over to Ireland, but didn't like what they saw and so handed over their share of the land to Ralegh. On hearing this, the Queen kindly gave Ralegh a troop of cavalry to keep the Irish in order, and a commander to lead them. The Munster state was enormous, and what with the lands he owned in Virginia, only the Queen owned more overseas lands than he.

Ralegh himself visited his estates in Munster only once in 1617 – the officer who commanded his cavalry there governed it for him. He never went to Virginia. He was always very good at choosing men to serve him who would be loyal and work in his best interests.

In the summer of 1587 Ralegh was concentrating on a great plan for his lands in the New World. He felt that it was all well and good to be called Lord and Governor of

Virginia, but one could count all the settlers there only too easily (there were only 18 of them) and they weren't real settlers – farmers and tradesmen – but just the soldiers Grenville had left there to defend Roanoke. What Virginia needed was a real city, which would draw people to live in it, and be a centre to which produce farmed in the surrounding countryside could be sent. Ralegh City – it sounded good.

The best place for the city, he decided, was just up the coast from Roanoke, in Chesapeake Bay, which John Lane already knew and said could be easily defended. By 7 January 1588 he had chosen a Governor for the new city, who would take his daughter and her husband with him, together with 89 other men, 17 women and 11 children. They sailed from Plymouth in May, but when they reached Roanoke in July they decided that it was too late for them to sail up to Chesapeake. There was a certain amount of trouble with the Indians – one of the settlers was brutally killed, hit by almost 20 arrows – but the settlers were optimistic. A little girl was born to one of the women, and named Virginia, the first English baby born in North America. Another was born only a few days later. The Governor Ralegh had appointed, John White, reported that all was well. Ralegh was delighted, and began to formulate all sorts of plans to encourage the new Virginians.

However, there was danger ahead, and he – and Drake – would soon have much more serious work to do.

Singeing the King's Beard

BY 1585, KING PHILIP had signed an agreement with Portugal, and the two countries' fleets were very likely to act together against England. Drake and Ralegh both argued that the Queen should strike first, but she hesitated to do so. English spies doubted whether Spain actually meant business. One wrote that there were rumours in Spain that the King:

> ...*will make a great army for England of 800 sail of ships, but as yet it seems but small preparation, and very unlikely*...

But then Philip suddenly commanded that all English ships in Spanish ports should be arrested, and their weapons and gunpowder taken onto his own ships. A small English ship, the *Primrose*, managed to escape from the Spanish and brought news of Spain's latest anti-English action to London, together with an actual piece of paper on which Philip's instructions had been written down. Elizabeth sent for Drake and sent him on a new expedition to the Caribbean. She let him know that there wouldn't be any objection to his laying his hands on any Spanish goods while he was there.

Drake had had all sorts of plans in his head for months, and didn't need much time to put one of them into action. He gathered together a large fleet and the Queen let him have two of her vessels, the *Elizabeth Bonadventure*, which carried almost 300 men, and the *Aid*, about half that size. The *Bonadventure* was a first-rate ship – *"the best-conditioned* [best-prepared] *ship in the world"*, one seaman thought her, and Drake made her his flagship. A number of the Queen's courtiers and friends supplied other ships, and a fleet of 25 – the largest ever to sail from an English port – set out from Plymouth on 14 September 1585. Eight days later they were off the coast of Spain, and Drake sent a message ashore demanding to know what the King meant by imprisoning English ships.

The Governor of the port of Bayona replied that he knew nothing about it, and asked if Drake would accept the present of some grapes, wine, bread and marmalade. Drake thought it was not worth attacking Bayona, and settled for being allowed to collect food and water for his ships, before sailing off to the Canary Islands, where he tried unsuccessfully to capture the town of Palma. This turned out to be well armed, and guns fired on his fleet – one cannon ball actually passed between Drake's legs as he stood on the deck of the *Elizabeth Bonadventure*. He sailed on to the Portuguese Cape Verdes islands, where he planned to take the town of Santiago.

On 17 November he landed with 1,000 men, and ordered a simultaneous attack from land and sea. The town fell into his hands with very little resistance. Unfortunately there was not much treasure to be found there and further bad luck followed when one of his crew caught typhus fever, which spread quickly through his ships so that within a few days nearly 300 men died. Many more were left weak and only just able to work the ships. They were certainly in no condition to fight. All the same, with those men who were fit, Drake took the city of Santo Domingo, on the island of Hispaniola – the oldest Spanish city in the area. Once again, there was none of the treasure he hoped for, but at least he was able to ransom the city – to persuade Spain to pay him to leave without burning the place to the ground.

Drake was not a man to let anyone get away with anything, and it was not a good idea to upset him. At Santo Domingo, a black boy, one of his cimarrons, was sent with a message to the Spaniards, under a flag of truce that should have kept him safe. But a Spaniard struck him with a lance and injured him so badly that he only just managed to stagger back before dying at Drake's feet. Drake immediately hanged two Spanish prisoners and said he would hang two more every day until the murderer of the boy was punished. The Spanish immediately hanged the man.

It was the end of January 1586 before the Spanish came to an agreement about the amount of ransom money to pay Drake to persuade him to leave Santo Domingo. He then turned his attention to Cartagena, smaller than Santo Domingo, but an important port, where the Spanish *flotas* called when they were both coming from Spain with supplies and returning with treasure. To take the city was not going to be easy, for the news of Drake's successes had circulated and the Governor had put almost 2,000 fighting men on galleys in the harbour, while 1,000 waited on land.

But the Spanish forces were not well commanded, and when Drake's force attacked, many of them, including the Governor, ran away. The English took the city with the loss of only 28 men. Drake thought of holding on to Cartagena and making it an English stronghold, but he could not spare the men necessary for such an undertaking, so he set about persuading the Spanish to hand over as much money as possible to ransom the city. They were slow to come to terms, and he had to set fire to a good many houses before they settled for something over £50,000 in the money of the time.

Drake sailed on to Roanoke, Ralegh's settlement – and, as we have already seen, took the settlers back with him to England. He had made about £65,000 on the voyage, £54,000 of it in treasure and the rest in cash. He had not only shown just how incapable Spain was of defending its cities in the Caribbean, but he had also cost the Spanish King an enormous amount in treasure and in money spent. No wonder William Cecil, now Lord Burghley, Elizabeth's Lord High Treasurer, remarked, *"Truly, Sir Francis Drake is a fearful man to the King of Spain."*

War was imminent. In 1585, the Queen's spies had uncovered a Catholic plot to assassinate her; and the result was the execution of Mary, Queen of Scots, Elizabeth's cousin, who supported it. To Drake, it was obvious that if Spain was going to invade England it would be soon – King Philip had been the husband of Elizabeth's sister, the last Queen, Mary. When Elizabeth died, he believed that he and the Scottish Queen Mary's son James would have an equal claim to the English throne. Elizabeth was now 52 years old – no longer a young woman. Drake certainly didn't care to remind her of that, but he never saw her now without arguing that he should be allowed to give the Spanish a final kick, before they could get a dangerous fleet together for an invasion.

His new fleet was even larger than the last: 24 ships and 3,000 men. He sailed quickly, on 2 April 1587. At the last minute the Queen grew worried that he might go rushing into Spanish harbours and actually start fighting on Spanish soil, and she sent a horseman galloping down to Plymouth with a letter forbidding him:

...to enter forcibly into any of the King's ports or havens, or to offer any violence to any of his towns or shipping within harbour or to do any act of hostility upon the land.

But it was too late; Drake had already set sail. With the wind behind him, he quickly came in sight of the port of Cadiz, in southern Spain, not far from Gibraltar and the entrance to the Mediterranean. In the harbour were 60 ships, most of them stocked with provisions – gunpowder and shot and other weapons – for the Armada that was to invade England. Drake approached quietly, then hoisted his flag and sailed right into the harbour. He captured many vessels, removed their cargoes and set the ships on fire; he also set fire to the great Spanish warship that belonged to the Marquis of Santa Cruz, the leader of the Armada. He later wrote to a friend:

The spectacle was very lamentable on their side; for many drowned themselves; many, half-burnt, leapt into the water; very many hanging by the ropes' ends by the ships' side, under the water even to the lips; many swimming with grievous wounds, strucken [hit] under water, and put out of their pain: and withal so huge a fire ... as, if any man had a desire to see Hell itself, it was there most lively figured.

Rear-Admiral Thomas Fenner, who commanded the *Dreadnaught*, reported to Sir Francis Walsingham, the

Queen's Secretary of State, that they had set fire to 20 large ships and many smaller ones, and sunk others. In all 38 had been destroyed and the English fleet had sailed off:

> ...*without the loss of any one man at the action, or any hurt, but only the master gunner of the Golden Lion, whose leg was broken by a great piece [cannon ball] from the town.*

Drake had well and truly *"singed the King of Spain's beard"*, as he said later. But as he sailed away from Cadiz he knew that what he had done was not enough to make a real difference to the risk of invasion. A great Armada of Spanish ships was still ready to attack. Now, before going home, he needed to get his hands on some treasure to help pay for the expedition. He sailed for a while along the coast of Portugal, destroying every ship he came across and landing his men now and then to burn down a few houses and monasteries (he and his men were always happy take any opportunity to annoy Catholics), but he found no treasure. Then, at the Azores, the Portuguese islands about 1,500 km west of Lisbon, he came across the *San Filipe*, the King of Spain's treasure ship. After a short, sharp battle, she surrendered, and Drake took her and her amazing cargo of gold, silver, pearls, spices. Back in Plymouth, he sent the Queen a special trunk containing some of the most magnificent pieces of treasure – golden chains and knives with golden handles, other gold ornaments, diamonds and rubies. It took 17 ships to carry the cargo from Plymouth to London, and its total value was said to be £112,000 (almost 27 million pounds today). The Queen took £50,000, the amount it cost her to run her whole Court for a year, and Drake was allowed to keep £20,000, amounting to 20 times the yearly income of a lord.

Perhaps more important was the news he gave the Queen – that no one had ever seen such a large force of seamen and soldiers as the army that the King of Spain had gathered together for the invasion of England.

One result of Drake's taking the *San Filipe* was that it frightened King Philip into sending a lot of his fleet to guard other treasure ships coming from the West Indies; the Armada he was getting together for the invasion of England was weakened and the invasion was postponed. But not for long.

Preparing for War

TWO OF THE MOST IMPORTANT JOBS the Queen had given Ralegh in 1585 were as Vice-Admiral of the West (making sure that all the warships stationed off the coasts of Devon and Cornwall were ready to fight) and Lord Lieutenant of Cornwall (inspecting the defences of the coastline of the two western counties, which were particularly threatened by Spain). He was also appointed to the War Council, where he sat with Drake, Sir Richard Grenville, his old friends "Black John" Norris and Ralph Lane (who had been given an appointment as General of the Forces), and the Governors of the islands of Guernsey and Wight.

Ralegh set up his headquarters in Plymouth, and set to work. For three years he and other officers concentrated on preparing for the fight that would certainly take place if the Spaniards managed to get their feet onto English soil. The south-west coast of England was the first piece of land an invading fleet from Spain would sight. In many places the high cliffs and dangerous rocks that made the coast so safe for smugglers, who knew them well and could take their small ships into little coves and estuaries impossible for larger ships, would make it almost impossible for Spaniards to land. But at some ports such as Falmouth, Plymouth, Dartmouth and Southampton, and on sandy beaches, a landing would be fairly easy.

Where there were beaches, stakes (large pointed poles) were set up, pointing towards the sea, and beacons were established all around the country. These were high poles up which flaming braziers could be hoisted, to send the news of an attack right across the country, from beacon to beacon, so that within minutes everyone would know of it. Ralegh had to make sure that the beacons were properly guarded. At Bath, one caught fire by accident and the whole countryside thought that the invasion had started. Ralegh knew that the watchmen must take special care that this did not happen again otherwise no one would believe the real warning when it came. So he arranged that no beacon could be lit unless a magistrate gave permission. Nobody attending a beacon was allowed to sit down (he might go to sleep), or to have a dog with him (he might be playing with the dog, and not notice that the next beacon along the coast had been lit). In some towns, watchmen were paid – at Launceston, near where

Drake was born, Jasper Bedlime was paid 11 pence *"to warn the parish that they should be ready at an hour's warning"*.

Ralegh also had to make sure that plenty of ammunition was in store near those places where the Spaniards would be most likely to land, and that the soldiers stationed nearby were well-trained and ready.

The Queen's father, Henry VIII, had built castles at St Mawes and Pendennis (overlooking the harbour of Falmouth), and St Nicholas's Island at Plymouth (now known as Drake's Island) was well fortified. The entrance to the harbour of Fowey was guarded by two small castles or blockhouses, and there was a chain that could be placed across the mouth of the harbour to prevent ships from entering it. There was a similar arrangement between Tilbury and Gravesend, to protect the Thames. St Michael's Mount, near Penzance, mounted guns looking out to sea. Watchtowers were built where Ralegh thought they were needed, but some ports were already well guarded. Falmouth and Plymouth were well-prepared, for they realized that King Philip's men would need to capture a good harbour before they could start unloading an army.

Next, the number of volunteer soldiers must be increased, and they must be properly trained. Training had only been taking place on two days a year, which was hardly sufficient to prepare an army for invasion. Captains were now ordered to travel around the country training groups of men ten times a year. The Spanish soldiers were used to fighting on land, and while England's seamen under Drake and others would look after any sea-battle, on land it would be another matter. Ralegh knew that if the Spaniards got a foothold, they would be difficult to stop.

He found the farmers and fishermen not at all eager to volunteer and train – they had enough to do just to scrape a living. The farmers were also upset when he explained that if the Spanish landed, they must be prepared to burn all their crops, so that the invaders could not harvest them and provide themselves with food. Some people simply refused to help.

There was a serious shortage of weapons. Guns were in short supply – and Ralegh was furious to hear that some English gun-makers were actually selling arms to the Spanish. He could not do much about that – it was perfectly legal, though it was done on the quiet – because it would not have made the guilty merchants very popular if it had been generally known. Bristol merchants sent nine shiploads of culverins (hand-guns) with gunpowder and shot through Naples to Spain, and a Sussex gun-maker sold England's enemy 100 cannon. One patriotic gun-maker, Ralph Hogge, told Sir Francis Walsingham that *"your enemy is better furnished with* [weapons] *than the ships of our own country are"*.

In one Cornish district, 1,008 men were prepared to fight but only 46 had pikes; in another only eight of 575 men were armed. Ralegh, with the help of local commanders such as Sir Richard Grenville, got to work, and within a few months, 3,988 longbows had been sent to Cornwall, with 2,973 sheaves [bundles] of arrows and 268 pikes. Cornwall, thanks to his efforts, ended up with an army of 5,560 well-armed men.

The people of the western counties were now growing nervous. In the summer of 1587 a fishing-boat hurried into harbour at Penzance and the skipper said he had seen a fleet of 150 ships just off the Scilly Isles. Most of the volunteers who would be called on to defend the coast were busy gathering the harvest, but were ready to drop their rakes and hurdles and pick up their pikes. However, it was a false alarm, and there was another in November, causing panic both at Falmouth and Plymouth. On neither occasion did anyone think of setting fire to the beacons, which worked out well under the circumstances, but would have been disastrous had the Spanish been invading for real.

Ralegh also went to East Anglia, up as far as King's Lynn, because though any ships coming from Spain would first sight the coast of Cornwall, any sailing from Holland, where King Philip had many boats ready, would aim for the coast of Norfolk. There was also an army of 17,000 men led by the Duke of Parma waiting just across the English Channel, ready to invade as soon as the Armada had made the Channel safe for them to cross. Just as he had done in the Westcountry Ralegh looked at those defences that were in place, argued for more, and made sure that weapons and ammunition – including large cannon – were going to be available as soon as they were needed.

Large numbers of soldiers were gathered in some places – at Tilbury, in Essex, for instance, which would defend the entrance of the river Thames, no fewer than 10,000 troops were gathered. These were professionals, and the Lieutenant-General of the army, Lord Hunsdon, had over 41,000 foot soldiers and 4,000 horsemen under his command.

Ralegh did not forget the coming war at sea and had readied his private warship. The four-masted *Bark Ralegh* was only two years old and one of the finest and most modern and finest vessels in the south-west. Three rows of guns looked out from her sides, and two more from her stern, at any other ship that ventured near her; she was fast, had a good, experienced crew, and was dangerous. Charles Howard, the Queen's Lord Admiral, thought her so fine that there was no other ship in which he would be so happy to sail. In 1587 Ralegh gave her to the Queen and re-named her *Ark Royal* – the first English ship to carry that name.

England was now as ready as Ralegh and the other officers of the Queen could make it, although on 7 June Lord Howard, the head of the Navy, wrote from Plymouth to Lord Burghley:

> *My good lord, there is here the gallantest company*
> *of captains, soldiers and mariners that I think ever*
> *was seen in England. And God send us the*
> *happiness to meet with [the Spaniards] before our*
> *men on land discover them, for I fear me a little sight*
> *of the enemy will fear the landmen much.*

There was much more Ralegh would like to have done,
given the time and the money. But for the moment, he
could only hope that the countrymen would keep a good
lookout, and stand by their beacons.

They did. On 19 July 1588, one beacon after another
flamed against the sky. The Spanish Armada had been
sighted in the Channel.

The Armada Sails

WHILE RALEGH HAD BEEN BUSY making sure the land defences were as strong as could be, Drake had been doing what he did best – preparing for a fight at sea. He knew the Armada, when it came, would be strong. In fact, it was stronger than even he could guess. One hundred and thirty-one Spanish ships set sail against England, carrying almost 25,000 soldiers and seamen, with 1,338 officers, 1,549 volunteers and 800 servants and priests (Spain was a very religious country, and all fighting men heard Mass before a battle).

Hakluyt, writing about the Armada some time later, described the largest and most dangerous ships:

> *The galleons were 64 in number, being of a huge bigness ... so high that they resembled great castles, most fit to defend themselves and to withstand any*

assault... [They] were rowed with great oars, there being in each one of them 300 slaves for that purpose... They were of such bigness that they contained within them chambers, chapels, turrets, pulpits and other commodities of great houses. All these were furnished and beautified [decorated] with trumpets, streamers, banners, warlike ensigns and other such like ornaments.

The size of the Spanish ships didn't matter. Few men knew more about fighting at sea than Drake, and he was especially keen on ships that were lighter but lower than the great Spanish galleons. The towers at each end of the galleons, in which the soldiers lived, often caught the wind and made the vessels slow and difficult to steer. Drake knew from experience that in the right conditions the faster English ships could run rings round them.

He was itching to set out and attack Spain rather than waiting for the Armada to sail against him, but the Queen was still hoping to avoid open war, and refused to give him permission. Meanwhile, down in Plymouth, he was exercising his crews to keep them from getting bored and careless. He was a little too enthusiastic about this, and Lord Howard of Effingham, the Lord Admiral of England, had to send him a message not to waste too much powder and shot on practice – especially after an accident in which one man was killed and another wounded. Howard told Sir Francis Walsingham, *"If you would write a word or two unto him to spare his powder, it would do well."*

Drake had been the first man Walsingham appointed to his War Council, and it was a good choice. He advised the Council that the English ships should keep their distance, firing at the ships across the water, rather than coming alongside for hand-to-hand fighting. He pointed out that by keeping away, the soldiers on the Spanish ships might just as well not be there, for all the harm they could do.

No one knew just when the attack would come. Ships sailed into port in England with rumour after rumour. On 7 June 1588 Drake wrote to London from *"on board Her Majesty's good ship the* Revenge, *riding in Plymouth Sound"* to say that a captain who had just returned from sea had seen:

...a great fleet of ships which came from Lisbon ... which the skipper and his company judge to be the great fleet that the King of Spain has made ready, for that they saw so many as they could not number them...

Too many to be counted! But it was another false alarm.

Waiting for the Spanish, the English fleet was divided into two. Up at Dover were 40 ships guarding the entrance to the river Thames, which led to London and the Queen herself. Down in Devon, Drake, under the command of Howard, was ready on his ship, the *Revenge*, with Sir John Hawkins nearby in the *Victory*, and almost 100 other ships lying in Plymouth Sound.

Everyone was getting very tense just hanging about waiting for something to happen. Drake still wanted to sail over to the Spanish coast and attack the Armada's ships while they were tied up in the harbours. In March, he wrote to the Queen arguing that he should be allowed to do just that. *"With 50 sail of shipping,"* he said, *"we shall do more good upon their own coast than a great many more will do here at home".*

The Queen sent for him to explain his plans more clearly. He had managed to persuade Howard that it would be right to go on the attack, and Effingham wrote to Walsingham saying that he, Drake, and the other commanders were quite certain:

> *...that the surest way to meet with the Spanish fleet is upon their own coast, or in any harbour of their own, and there to defeat them.*

Together, they managed to convince the Queen, and she gave Howard and Drake permission to set out for Spain. Unfortunately bad weather, so often his enemy, held them up for three weeks, and when they managed to get out of harbour they spent a week fighting against the winds and waves rather than the Spanish, and in the end had to return to Plymouth just in time to hear that Spanish ships had been seen near the Scilly Isles. Had the Armada sailed this time? But no, the next thing they heard, the Spanish ships seemed to be sailing back towards Spain! Drake thought that they had probably been damaged by the very storm that he and Howard had been fighting, and on 4 July he set out after them.

Bad weather was once again against him, and not finding any sign of the Spanish ships Drake and Howard had no idea of the best course of action. Drake was rowed across from the *Revenge* to Howard's flagship, the *Ark Royal*, and they held a council of war. Drake persuaded Howard that they should go on – he thought now that since the Armada probably hadn't actually sailed, they might (as they'd planned) be able to discover and destroy it wherever it lay at anchor. But the wind stopped blowing when they were only 100 km from the Spanish coast, and they had to turn again for England.

On that very day – 19 July – the Spanish fleet at last set sail for England, under the command of the splendidly named Don Alonzo Pérez de Guzmán el Buono, Duke of Medina Sidonia and King Philip's Captain of the High Seas. He was a courageous but gentle, quiet man, and not at all keen to sail against England. He told the King that he was not at all well, had no experience of fighting at sea – in fact, no experience of fighting – added to which he always suffered badly from seasickness. But the King insisted, and he found himself on his way into battle.

Sidonia had a rough journey, and he spent a lot of it lying down in his cabin. Many of the troops on board his ships were seasick, too, especially when the fleet was hit by bad weather. That didn't matter too much though – until they could get to land, it was the seamen who were important, and seasickness didn't bother them!

Ralegh

The Great Half Moon

19 July 1588

AT 4 PM ON 19 JULY 1588, Captain Thomas Fleming, an English pirate, was sailing his ship the *Golden Hind* around the Channel looking for some helpless vessel to capture (he was actually wanted for stealing goods from another English ship). Suddenly he saw, in the distance, a crowd of ships sailing towards England. As they drew nearer, he saw huge red crosses on their sails. The ships were large, and sailing in formation *"like a half moon, the 'wings thereof spreading out about the length of seven miles"*. The Spaniards were on their way to invade England!

Warned by Ralegh's beacons, a great crowd of people – the Mayor, the councillors and others – came to the Hoe (the hill above Plymouth that looks out over the sea) and saw in the distance Sidonia's great Spanish fleet sailing up-channel in a half-circle.

At his headquarters at Portland Castle, on the Dorset coast, Ralegh knew he had done all that was humanly possible to protect his country. He watched anxiously to see what course the Armada would take: would Sidonia turn in towards the coast and attempt a landing? No, he sailed on up-channel.

Everyone must have been surprised at the number of ships – nine enormous Portuguese galleons, 10 smaller ones, four support ships, four Italian galleasses (heavy, low ships), 42 armed merchant ships and over 50 other vessels carrying supplies, including gunpowder and shot, with smaller boats tagging along behind, which could be used for taking messages between the larger vessels.

But they were heartened as they watched Howard's fleet sail out to meet the enemy – Howard himself on his flagship, the *Ark Royal*, Drake on the *Revenge*, followed by the *Elizabeth Jonas*, the *Hope*, the *Triumph*, *White Bear*, *Foresight*, *Dreadnaught*, *Swiftsure* and the rest. Ralegh was enough of a seaman to know that it would be difficult to get the English fleet out of harbour: the wind was in the wrong direction, and the tide was coming in. In fact, Howard's ships had to wait until the tide had turned, and then use small boats to tow the larger ships out of the harbour.

The English Navy, Ralegh had been telling everyone who would listen, was now the best in the world. If Drake had more practical experience at sea, Ralegh was perhaps more experienced in planning, in persuading other men to accept new ideas in the design of ships, the layout of guns, and so on. He and Hawkins had thoroughly modernized the design of England's ships. As he watched the puffs of smoke and heard the distant thump of guns as the first shots were fired, he knew that what was coming would be a great test for ships and men. He also knew that the Spanish side was stronger, for England had only 51 ships of over 200 tons, while Spain had 93. But if the English ships were fewer and smaller, they were faster, and their gunners were quicker about their duties. And because the English guns were smaller than the Spanish, they could be moved more quickly and were easier to re-load and fire.

Ralegh was impatient that the only thing he could do now was stand on shore and look on. The Queen had refused him permission to join one of the ships and take part in the coming battle.

Drake
The First Shot
19 – 25 July 1588

WHEN CAPTAIN FLEMING saw the sails of the Armada in the distance, he set out for Plymouth Sound as fast as he could go and told Sir Francis Drake that he had seen the Spanish Armada near the Scilly Isles. Drake, so the story goes, was playing a quiet game of bowls on Plymouth Hoe. He turned to one of his men, William Page, and gave him £5 to take the news to the Queen in London and then, when he saw that everyone expected him to dash away to the *Revenge* and set sail, said: *"We have time enough to finish the game and beat the Spaniards too"*

The story may or may not be true, but it certainly sounds right: Drake was absolutely sure that he could beat the largest Armada the Spanish could send against him, though looking out from Plymouth at the great fleet of slow, huge ships, it must have seemed almost as if three-quarters of the world was sailing against England. Even Drake must surely have been as surprised as Ralegh at the size of the fleet, as he sailed out to meet it.

No one knows exactly what happened during the next day or two. Everyone was far too busy fighting to make notes of who was where, and fighting whom. Those on-shore had to rely on muddled accounts given by word of mouth or by rough notes written by captains who for a lot of the time had very little idea what was going on anywhere except just where they happened to be. As a result, historians still argue about exactly how the battle against the Armada was fought and won.

We do know how it started. Howard, in command of the English fleet, ordered the *Disdain*, one of the smallest, fastest ships he had, to dart in towards the Spanish ships, fire the first shot of the battle across the bows of the Spanish Admiral's flagship, and then nip quickly out again. Then, at 9 AM, battle commenced. For four hours the ships of the two fleets exchanged shots, but uncertain of how close they dared to get to each other, did very little damage at first.

At the end of the first day, the Spanish had a piece of very bad luck. One of their ships ran into another, and both were damaged. Then a third, the *San Salvador*, exploded – something had set off the gunpowder in her hold. She burst into flame, and over 200 of the 319 troops on board were killed or jumped overboard and were drowned.

During the night, Drake followed the *San Rosario*, one of the ships that had been damaged in the collision. She was one of the most impressive and powerful vessels in the whole Armada, with no fewer than 46 guns on board, but she was in a bad way, and on the morning of 30 July Drake sailed close to her and demanded her surrender. The captain, Don Pedro de Valdes, recognising "El Draque", immediately had himself and some of his officers rowed to the *Revenge*. Drake greeted them with a fanfare of trumpets, and gave a banquet in his cabin, after which Don Pedro surrendered cheerfully to, he said *"the greatest seaman of the age"*. An official report said that:

> *...the said Don did say and give out in speech that since it was his chance to be taken he was glad that he fell into Sir Francis Drake's hands.*

Drake was once again a pirate, capturing an impressive warship for which he could claim a great deal of prize money. He sent the *Rosario* into Dartmouth. (Later he would be especially pleased when he found out just how much she was worth – she carried a large treasure chest.) The other English captains may well have been jealous, for there were going to be rich pickings for Drake and his crew. But everyone else was delighted, and when the news of the *Rosario's* capture reached London, bonfires were lit in celebration.

On 23 July both fleets were off Portland Bill, ready for a second battle. The largest English ship, the *Triumph*, attacked a group of Spanish ships, and as she began to get the better of them, other Spanish captains rushed forward to help their countrymen. Drake, seeing this, hurried in and attacked so violently that the Spanish ships *"were all forced to give way"*, as Howard said, admiringly.

But the danger was not over: the English ships had fired so many shots that they were almost out of ammunition. And the Spanish Armada was still, though battered, sailing on up the Channel. When they looked closely, the English saw that they had not actually done much damage, even to the *San Martin*, at which they had been concentrating much of their fire. Their cannon balls were too light to wreck such heavy ships, and the big Spanish vessel had only lost some of her rigging.

Drake realized that he had to stop the Armada within the next day or two if possible, before it reached the Isle of Wight. If the Spanish captured the island, they would probably be able to go on and take the ports of Portsmouth and Southampton. Crowds were already gathering on the cliffs as the Armada came in sight, to watch the coming fight. Drake was determined not to let England down in front of them.

He had enjoyed some victories, but he hadn't so far been able to stop the Armada. Now he came in from the south, attacking the Spanish with all guns, hoping to drive the Spanish ships, or at least some of them, on to the Owers Banks — treacherous sandbanks along the coast. In fact, he was trying to run the Armada aground.

Just in time, the commander of the Spanish fleet, Medina Sidonia, realized what Drake was up to, and managed to avoid going aground on the sandbanks near Selsey Bill. He ordered the Armada to turn away from the coast, and they sailed safely on up-channel to Calais.

RALEGH STILL WANTED to be part of the battle of the Armada. He must have realized that whoever won and lost, it was going to be remembered as one of the great moments in England history, and he was missing it! He must have been very tempted just to get on board the *Ark Royal* – his ship, after all – and sail out to battle. It was maddening that she should be leading the English fleet into the fight without him on board. But to disobey the Queen's orders on such an important occasion would have been a very serious matter indeed. Men had been beheaded for less.

In spite of that, in the end he couldn't resist. A man who had for far too long been refused permission by the Queen to do anything but ride about the country organizing things, he wanted a piece of the action. On 28 July, he finally decided that the time had come to stop organizing, and actually do something. He left Portland Castle and rushed up to London, begging the Queen to let him serve her at sea. She sympathized at last, and sent him off with a message to Lord Howard on the *Ark Royal*. Back at the coast, he leaped into a small boat, was taken out to the commander's ship, and at last joined the fight.

Ralegh played his part in planning the next stage of the battle. The English ships were still short of gunpowder and shot, and as both sides paused to take a breather the English commanders – Ralegh, Drake, Hawkins and Howard – met on board the *Ark Royal* to decide what to do next. Fire-ships, they thought, were the best chance of damaging the Spanish fleet. Drake had seen these in action against him at San Juan de Ulua, and had used them against the Spanish at Cadiz.

So, just before midnight, eight English ships were prepared to sail with the tide towards Calais harbour, where most of the Armada ships had moored in what they thought was safety. The crews were taken off the English ships, and they were packed with barrels of pitch and tar, and any explosives which could be spared. A few men on each made sure that the sails were properly set and the rudders tied, so that they were pointing in the right direction; then they set fire to fuses which would carry flames to the pitch and tar barrels, scrambled over the sides, and rowed back to the other ships waiting a short distance away.

There was a good wind, and in no time the fire-ships had covered the two kilometres to the harbour. They had been well aimed: six of the seven sailed in among the Spanish fleet, and the fires on board burst into full flame. The fire should have spread to the Spanish ships as they collided, and in no time the harbour would have been ablaze with burning vessels, the gunpowder in the Spanish ships' holds exploding and blowing them to pieces.

It didn't happen, because the fire-ships didn't actually collide with any Spanish ships, but just ran aground and burned out. However, the raid was a success anyway because of the confusion it caused. A few Spanish vessels – including Sidonia's own ship – escaped by hurriedly lifting their anchors and getting away from the danger area, but others collided with each other, and the Spanish flagship, the *San Lorenzo*, ran ashore. A naval lieutenant described how:

...the soldiers leaped overboard and fled to the shore, swimming and wading. Some escaped with being wet, some – and that very many – were drowned.

Lord Howard ordered his men to board the stranded *San Lorenzo*, and successfully captured the ship – though the Governor of Calais then insisted that as she was aground on the French coast, the English had no right to her, and actually fired on them so that they had to leave her.

Other ships managed to get out to sea, but the Armada was no longer a dangerous group of ships waiting to act together against the enemy, but separate vessels scattered along the coast, unable to contact each other, and with no idea what was going on.

Back in London, the Queen was anxiously waiting for news. Messages were slow to reach her, and when they did she could not be absolutely sure that they were accurate. She had received two letters from Drake warning her that he thought the Spanish ships were being repaired, and that there was still a chance of an attack. The Army must be kept ready.

The main force was still at Tilbury, and a church-warden from Lambeth had visited the Army, and reported that the men were looking forward to a good fight, and that when they heard rumours that the Spanish troops were on their way, *they were as joyful at such news as if lusty giants were about to run a race*.

On 10 August, the Queen was told that Parma's army was on its way towards England, and decided to go down to Tilbury to encourage her army. She walked into the middle of her troops with only four men and two boys to guard her – an Earl carrying the huge Sword of State, a page in white velvet carrying a silver helmet with a white plume, another boy leading a charger. The Earl of Leicester, Captain General of the army, was on her right hand, and the Earl of Essex on her left. Behind her was one more elderly courtier, Sir John Norreys.

She mounted her horse so that she could be seen and heard by at least some of the 5,000-strong army, and made the most famous speech of her life to her *"faithful and loving people"*. She was determined, she said, to live or die among them. Then she went on:

> *I know I have but the body of a weak and feeble woman; but I have the heart and stomach of a King, and of a King of England, too, and think it foul scorn that Parma or Spain or any Prince of Europe should dare to invade the borders of my realm; to which, rather than any dishonour should grow by me, I myself will take up arms.*

She could not do that, of course, and everyone knew it. But it was a wonderful speech, and they cheered her long and loud.

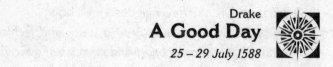

Drake
A Good Day
25 – 29 July 1588

IN THE AFTERMATH of the fire-ship attack, the Spanish
tried to tempt Drake to come in and tackle them in hand-
to-hand fighting. But he wisely kept his distance, darted
in and out among the larger, slower vessels in his quicker
ships, and did them enormous damage at close quarters.
Soon the decks of the *San Felipe* and the *Maria Juan*
were piled with dead and wounded men, and they and
the *San Mateo* were so badly damaged that they had to
retreat. The *Maria Juan* was almost sinking.

Many stories were told on both sides about the battle.
One survivor from the *Maria Juan* told how the
commander's head had been taken clean off by one shot,
and how:

> ...*where I and four others were trimming our
> foresail [working to fold up a sail], there came a*

bullet and struck away the shoe of one of us without doing any other harm.

A sailor on Drake's *Revenge* described how:

That day Sir Francis Drake's ship was pierced through by several cannon balls of all sizes which were flying everywhere between the two fleets . . . His cabin was twice pierced by cannon balls and there was an occasion in which two gentlemen, towards evening, had retired to rest a little after the battle, and one of them lying upon the bed when it was broken to pieces under him by a ball, without his taking the least hurt. And shortly afterwards the Earl of Cumberland ... and Sir Charles Blount were resting on the same bed in the same place when it was again hit by a ball which passed through the cabin from one side to the other without doing any harm other than scrape the foot, taking off the toes of one who was there with them.

During the battle 1,500 Spanish men had been killed or drowned, and hundreds wounded. Four ships had been lost – two sunk, two driven aground – and many others were seriously damaged. Sidonia cried out to one of his commanders, *"What shall we do? We are lost."* Drake wrote to Walsingham, *"God hath given us a good day"*.

He was ordered to drive on behind the scattered Spanish ships as they turned from the channel towards the North Sea. He knew that those ships were full of men who were tired from fighting and weak from the bad food and stale water that they had to eat and drink. But the English sailors were not a lot better off, and he was afraid of disease. Typhus fever had already broken out on some of Howard's ships. The sooner they could get ashore and take on fresh supplies, the better.

The weather, so often against him, turned in his favour this time: storms blew up that were so strong that he could not follow the Spaniards up towards Scotland, as he had intended. He turned back, and on 8 August landed at Margate. There, many of his men did fall sick and die, often from food poisoning. The Government was slow in paying them, so they could not leave their ships, and lay in filthy conditions. Howard wrote to the Privy Council complaining that:

> ...*most part of the fleet is grievously infected, and men die daily, falling sick in the ships by numbers, and the ships themselves be so infectious as it is thought to be a very plague.*

Drake was furious, too, and went up to London with Howard to beg for money to care for the sick and wounded; but they got none. They paid out some money from their own purses to the sailors who were worst off.

Drake was now a national hero – even an international one. The whole world seemed to have heard of him. Even the Pope in Rome, hearing of the defeat of the Armada, said: *"What courage! Do you think he showed any fear? He is a great captain."*

Because he was so well known as a pirate and a round-the-world sailor, and because of his bravery, he got much more attention and praise than the other captains, who were often more than a little annoyed. Sir Martin Frobisher, who had played an important part in the fight, was especially upset. Drake, he said, was going around saying that nobody had fought the Spaniards but he, but *"he shall well understand that others have done as good service as he, and better too."*

The misunderstandings and arguments went on for a while, and disagreements about who should have shares in the prize money went on much longer. But the battle itself was over. Back home, Drake proudly carried back to Plymouth the medal the Queen had struck to commemorate the victory. On it were words from the Bible, in Latin, which in English read *"God blew and they were scattered"*. Many people believed that God, on the side of the English, had raised a storm to destroy the Armada.

You might think that it was now time for a little peace and quiet, but Drake was never one to sit at home. There would be – there must be – more adventures ahead.

Married and Banished

OVER THE NEXT TWO MONTHS, there were fierce storms off the coasts of Scotland and western Ireland. Up in the north sea and beyond, Sidonia's battered fleet tried desperately to get home. The *Girona* sank off the Giant's Causeway with the loss of over 1,000 men. The *Santa Maria de la Rosa* went on the rocks and only one man escaped drowning; the *Gran Grin* went ashore on the Irish coast and the few members of the crew who struggled ashore were murdered by the Irish – the English Lord Deputy of Ireland had ordered his men to kill any Spaniard found alive on shore. More ships went down nearby. It was said that over 1,200 bodies were counted on one beach in the bay of Donegal.

Medina Sidonia led a small procession of tattered vessels into harbour at Santander, in northern Spain. Hundreds of sick men staggered on to land – 180 men had died during the voyage on Sidonia's own flagship.

Ralegh watched as so many of the broken ships of the great Spanish Armada crashed onto the rocks of Ireland. The Queen sent him off on one of her ships to report on what was going on. He was put in command of 700 soldiers, just in case any Spanish soldiers managed to land in Ireland. They weren't needed. *"A great many of the crews of the Spanish fleet were crushed against the rocks,"* Ralegh later wrote:

> *...and those that landed, being very many in number, were notwithstanding broken, slain and taken prisoner, and so sent from village to village in halters to be shipped into England.*

You might think that everyone would be so relieved that for the time at least the danger from Spain was over, that personal quarrels would be forgotten, but this was not the case. By the end of 1589, when Ralegh returned to Court, all sorts of squabbles and jealousies arose, and Queen Elizabeth herself stirred things between Ralegh and his great rival Essex.

She seemed determined to make them quarrel: one day she seemed to favour Ralegh, the next his younger rival. She made Essex a Knight of the Garter – a great honour – though he had not done nearly as much as Ralegh in preparing for the Armada. A little while later, however, she sent Ralegh a valuable gold chain, which Essex thought he deserved much more than his rival. At one point, Essex actually challenged Ralegh to a duel. This would have meant trouble for both of them: if they fought each other it would be goodbye to the Court and the Queen's favour, so they just exchanged insults and did their best to avoid each other. For a while Ralegh went off to Ireland to look after his estates there, but when he heard that a courtier had been putting it about that *"My Lord of Essex has chased Mr Ralegh from court"*, he quickly returned.

In need of money he decided to turn pirate again. In 1591 he fitted out a fleet of 12 ships to sail off to the Azores (where Drake had captured the prize *San Filipe* in 1586) and lie in wait for Spanish treasure ships. He meant to go himself on board his own ship, the *Black Dog*, but once again the Queen decided she could not spare him, and Sir Richard Grenville took his place, on the *Revenge*. When they reached their destination, Ralegh's ships met with a group of new ships that King Philip had built – in the manner of the small, swift English ships that had defeated the Armada. Cut off from the rest of the English ships, Grenville refused to turn away from the Spanish, and for almost 24 hours the *Revenge* was battered, until Grenville himself was mortally wounded, and at last the *Revenge* was captured.

When news reached Ralegh back in England, he wrote an account of the battle that has become one of the greatest pieces of English writing about war at sea. He hadn't been anywhere near the battle, but his account of it was so vivid that everyone was soon talking about it – as we might today talk about a filmed television report of a battle. It impressed the Queen so much that in January 1592 she actually gave him a castle – Sherborne, in Dorset, with a large amount of land around it – or at least almost gave it to him; he had a lease for 99 years, and only had to pay £360 rent a year. No wonder that in return he gave her a jewel worth £250!

The present was just in time. A little while later he would earn the Queen's displeasure, and fall dramatically from favour. She didn't know that he was in love with one of her maids of honour, the beautiful and intelligent Elizabeth Throckmorton. They had known each other for some time – she had been at court since she was 20, and they must have seen each other almost every day when Ralegh was in London.

Courting one of the Queen's maids of honour was a dangerous thing to do. She ran her Court like a strict girls' school, and if any man dared to make eyes at one of "her" women, it was the worse for him. Unfortunately, Ralegh and Bess Throckmorton couldn't help themselves; they fell head over heels in love, and were soon meeting secretly. She soon found herself pregnant, and in November 1592 they were secretly married. It wasn't a case of Ralegh "doing the right thing" – they really were in love, and really wanted to be married – but they both knew how the Queen would react when she found out that Ralegh, her great favourite, had given himself to another woman. He certainly remembered that his rival Essex had got into great trouble for secretly marrying two years earlier – Elizabeth had been furious, and had banished him from Court.

Of course Ralegh and Bess couldn't hope to keep their own marriage secret for long – one of the main pleasures at Court was gossip. He knew that the best he could expect was to be sent away from Court. If he managed to carry off a really successful raid – capture a Spanish treasure ship, for instance – she would surely forgive him?

He told the Queen that he was determined to avenge the death of Grenville, and bring her treasure, and spent over £10,000 – almost two and a half million pounds today – on preparing an expedition. But once again she refused to give him permission to sail to the Carribbean, although he managed to persuade her to let him go as far as the coast of Spain with the fleet. On 29 March 1592, while he was in Cornwall waiting to sail, his son was born.

For a while, the news was kept from the Queen – in fact, less than a month after the birth, Bess went back to Court as though nothing had happened. Ralegh sailed for Spain, but a stern message suddenly followed from the Queen. He was to return to London immediately.

If he had been a little more tactful, he might have got away without too much trouble. He should have gone to the Queen and grovelled, apologizing for deceiving her. He and the Queen were, after all, old friends. But he didn't – and neither did Bess. Elizabeth wouldn't put up with behaviour like that, and on 7 August Ralegh and Bess were sent to the Tower of London.

What got Ralegh out again, after only five weeks, was the arrival back in Plymouth of the fleet with which he had hoped to sail, with a rich prize, the *Madre de Dios*, a Portuguese ship coming back to Spain from the East Indies with more treasure on board than any ship yet captured by an English pirate. Tons of spices, pepper, cloves, nutmeg, ebony, jewels, ivory, silver, gold – possibly worth, altogether, as much as half a million pounds then – a hundred and twenty million today.

The *Madre de Dios* was brought into Dartmouth, and the moment the news got round the local people more or less rioted. They crowded onto the ship and started making off with whatever they could lay their hands on – and many of the crew were too busy doing the same thing to stop them. Soon, men were swapping gold nuggets or diamonds for beer in the local pubs. As the news travelled further, men came from all over the Westcountry, many bringing horses and carts to carry off as much treasure as they could. Soon, jewellers started arriving from as far away as London, eager to steal diamonds, rubies, gold – or to buy them cheaply from others who had stolen them. It was said that over 2,000 men were in Dartmouth robbing or trying to rob the ship.

The only man who knew exactly how the profits from the ship's capture should be shared out among the people who had put money into the expedition, and was feared enough in the Westcountry to be able to control the looting, was Ralegh. So he was taken from the Tower (though under close guard) and sent down to Dartmouth. He saw a chance to get back in the Queen's good books, and swore that nobody would get away with anything if he could prevent it:

> *If I meet any of them coming up, I mean to strip them as naked as ever they were born, for it is infinite [certain] that Her Majesty has been robbed of the most rare things.*

He said he could actually smell the spices which they had stolen and hidden in their pockets.

When he arrived, Ralegh was greeted with cheers by members of his old crews, and in no time at all had things under control.

The Queen didn't show a lot of gratitude, taking most of the profits from the *Madre de Dios*, while the men who had put money into the venture – including Ralegh – got very little. And the moment he had finished getting things in order at Dartmouth, he was taken back to the Tower. He and his wife were released in time for Christmas 1592 – but they didn't spend it, as usual, at Court, with all the feasting and fun the Queen so much enjoyed. Instead, they had to go down to Sherborne, where Ralegh set about putting the castle in order, making repairs.

Their baby had died whilst in the Tower but in 1593 a son was born, and though Ralegh thought from time to time about life at Court, for the time he was happy with Bess and little Wat.

To Arms, to Arms

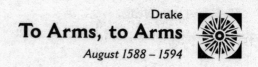

August 1588 – 1594

THE QUEEN'S ADVISERS were all keen to follow up the destruction of the Armada with another great blow against Spain. With any luck, England's great enemy could be so badly injured that the war would be won, and all fear of invasion banished for good.

But the Queen had been dithering. After her death, Ralegh wrote:

> *If the late Queen had believed her men of war ... we had in her time beaten that great empire in pieces and made their kings kings of figs and oranges... But Her Majesty did all by halves and by petty invasions taught the Spaniard how to defend himself, and to see his own weakness which, till our attempts taught him, was hardly known to himself.*

But at least, in 1589, she agreed to a plan Drake had made with Burghley, the Lord High Treasurer. Those Spanish ships that had actually managed to struggle back to port in Spain must be destroyed, Lisbon should be captured, and so should the islands of the Azores. This last point was particularly important, because it was the best place from which to capture the *flotas* or treasure-ship fleets.

Drake set about getting ships together, with an old friend from his days in Ireland, Sir John Norris – "Black John" – who was on the War Council with himself and Ralegh. On 23 February Drake received his official orders. His most important task was to take the Azores, but he was also to attack the ports of Santander, San Sebastian and Corunna, and destroy any Armada ships anchored there, then go on to attack Spanish-controlled Lisbon.

Drake and Black John were particularly keen on attacking Lisbon. Drake had become friendly with Dom Antonio, a nobleman with a claim to the throne of Portugal. He was already calling himself King, and said he would be a friend of England if Drake could help him to the crown. Elizabeth was doubtful, but Drake thought it an excellent idea. The Portuguese were now rebelling against Spain, and might be happy to welcome Dom Antonio.

Drake sailed in the middle of April on the *Revenge*, leading 180 ships with over 4,000 sailors, carrying 13,000 soldiers. There was great excitement and enthusiasm about the project which, it was hoped, would deal a final blow against the Spanish. One patriotic poet, George Peele, put it into words: *"To arms, to arms, to glorious arms! You fight for Christ and England's peerless queen!"*

On one of the ships travelled the excited Dom Antonio, with a splendid suit of bullet-proof black armour, which he intended to wear when he stepped ashore on "his" kingdom to claim "his" crown.

Drake made for the Spanish port of Corunna, where there were said to be many Armada ships. When he got there, he found only a few, but he landed a small army that easily captured the town, and then ran through it burning, looting and taking great quantities of food (biscuits and beef, fish and corn).

By the time they sailed on to Lisbon many members of his crew had begun to suffer from a mystery illness, and many soldiers of the army with which Black John marched on Lisbon were also sick and weak. His attack on the city failed, partly because though Dom Antonio expected to be welcomed with open arms, nobody showed a great deal of interest in putting him on the throne. He hoped and expected many Portuguese to come over to his side, but they didn't. The only people to meet him, a member of the army said, were:

> ...*a company of poor peasants, without hose [stockings] or shoes, and one gentlewoman who presented the King with a basket of cherries and plums.*

The Portuguese weren't at all keen on Dom Antonio, and they hated the English Protestants more than they hated the Spanish.

Drake realized there was nothing to do now but get back to England. It was a sad and sorry fleet that limped into port. The sickness had killed many sailors and soldiers. On one ship, the *Dreadnaught*, only three men out of 300 were healthy and over 100 had died. On the *Griffin* there were *"none that were well and able to hoist a sail, and there were not in the ship five or six men well."* Perhaps 10,000 men had died from the mystery sickness, which was probably some sort of plague.

For the first time in his life, Drake had failed. He hadn't taken Lisbon; he hadn't reached the Azores. It was not his fault: if the Portuguese had supported Dom Antonio, and he had been set on the throne as he had hoped, and if the sickness had not struck Drake's men ... but it was no use sitting thinking out excuses. He must have wondered what sort of greeting he would get from the Queen. Fortunately, she was not angry – in fact she congratulated him on what he had managed to achieve in the face of such setbacks.

Back home at Buckland Abbey, Drake hung up on the wall the drum that had gone with him on most of his voyages, and on which his drummer had beaten his crews into action, and settled down for almost six years to look after local affairs. The years between 1589 and

1594 weren't wasted. Far from it; it seemed as though almost every week he got long letters and documents from London asking his advice on various matters. He became a magistrate and a Member of Parliament, working particularly on behalf of the poor and sick seamen who had served their country well and had then been forgotten. When the Government wasn't enthusiastic, he and Hawkins set up a scheme whereby sailors paid some of their wages into a fund to help their less fortunate brothers.

Drake also kept a firm eye on the defences of the Devon and Cornwall coast. The threat of a Spanish invasion might be less than it once was, but it was still not impossible that the Spanish might have another go. He saw that plenty of arms were stored in Plymouth, that the town was well protected, and that some old ships in the harbour were loaded with tar so that they could be turned into fire-ships if need be.

One of his greatest achievements was to make sure that the town had a good supply of fresh water. This was very important – not only so that the people of the town had fresh water to drink, but also to ensure that there was plenty to supply the ships that needed it. The rivers which flowed into the sea at the town were polluted. Drake organized the building of a leat or stream, six feet wide and two feet deep, for 27 km from Meavy, in the country, to the city. When the task was finished, and the first water began to flow, a trumpeter on horseback rode like the wind along the whole length of the leat to announce its arrival at Plymouth. Every year for at least 200 years a ceremony was held in August when the Mayor and Corporation of Plymouth drank water from the leat in honour of Sir Francis Drake.

Ralegh
Golden Men, Walking
1594 – 1595

FOR A WHILE, RALEGH, like Drake, was happy to forget the
Court and the Queen. He settled down to country
amusements at Sherborne: hunting, meeting with his
neighbours, planting gardens, looking after his estate, and
writing poetry.

He did not forget the Spanish threat, though, and made
several speeches pointing out that the danger of a Spanish
attack was not yet over – though he was also trading with
Spain, selling timber from his estates in Ireland to the
Spanish islands of Madeira and the Canaries. Despite the
fact that England and Spain were still at war, trade still
went on between the two countries; Englishmen would
have been sorry to give up Spanish sherry and sweet wines.

His attempts to colonize Virginia had been more or less
a failure. There was still only a token force of men there
rather than a thriving settlement, and his estates in Ireland

were not doing as well as he had hoped (he would eventually sell them all off). Increasingly he found his thoughts turning to the stories he had heard seven years ago from the Spaniard Sarmiento de Gamboa – the stories of El Dorado, the city of gold. It sounded like a dream: a place where, it was said, the knives and forks, the saucepans and frying pans were all of gold, and where the King had a garden in which life-sized golden models of the country's animals sat about under golden trees and bushes. On special occasions the King and his chief ministers covered themselves with oil and then had their bodies powdered with gold dust. Golden men, walking about! Was it possible?

Ralegh could not stop thinking about El Dorado, and how he might get there. It sounded as though the greatest pirate treasure of all was there to be taken! If he could only get an expedition together – even if he didn't find the golden city, he could pay for the voyage by capturing a treasure ship or two. He might now be 40 years old, but he was still a pirate at heart.

In 1594, Ralegh sent a single ship, commanded by an old friend, Jacob Whiddon, to do some research around the Orinoco River in Venezuela. Most of the people Ralegh could find who said they knew something about El Dorado seemed to think that it was somewhere in the valley where that river ran. Whiddon came back saying that the natives he had spoken to certainly believed that a great golden city did exist, and Ralegh was able to go to the Queen and ask for permission to explore the area on her behalf. She agreed, and even added that at the same time he should annoy the Spanish in any way he could.

The fleet that Ralegh got together in the Westcountry was one full of pirates, with himself as leader. It included Amyas Preston, George Somers, George Popham, Sir Robert Dudley and John Grenville. Drake knew them all, and though they might have been rivals in the past, he knew they were as keen on gold as he was himself. In February 1595 about 150 men sailed on five ships. Ralegh – who had never had the chance to sail himself and had had to sit at home while others had all the excitement – was delighted to be crossing the Atlantic for the first time. He had had enough of staying at home playing courtier to the Queen.

In May, he and 100 of his men set off in rowing boats up the Orinoco, the great river that flowed for 2,000 km from its source to the Atlantic, and in places was 50 km wide. They had a hard time of it: as Ralegh wrote later, they were:

> ...all driven to lie in the rain and weather in the open air, in the burning sun, and upon hard boards... What with the victuals [food] being mostly fish, with the wet clothes of so many men thrust together and the heat of the sun, I will undertake there was never any prison in England that could be found more unsavoury and loathsome.

It was a great adventure, all the same. They pushed on into thick forest where no Englishman had ever been, seeing brightly coloured birds and flowers few white men had ever seen. But it was tough going. The current was strong, and the heat and lack of good food exhausted them. The river was full of crocodiles, so they could not even refresh themselves by taking a swim.

After 15 days they saw mountains. Surely El Dorado must lie ahead? The natives certainly had stories of a strange country where men in bright red cloaks wore ornaments of gold. And they found a few tools that suggested the Spanish had been there before them and perhaps found buried gold. But the party was just too exhausted to go on. Ralegh was convinced that he had reached a part of the world where there was gold to be mined, and other minerals too; the expedition had been successful in finding a way up-river that could be used again. The party turned, and went back to their ships.

Ralegh's only disappointment was that he had found no treasure ships to capture, and when he sailed back into English waters, he could not claim that he had raised enough money to begin to pay for the expedition. He was furious when some people actually began saying that he had not been to the Orinoco at all – he had been sitting down in Devon all the time, and was making the whole thing up.

He hastily wrote a book about the adventure, with a long but eye-catching title: *The Discovery of the Large, Rich and Beautiful Empire of Guinea with a Relation of the*

Great and Golden City of Manoa. Though a bestseller and such an exciting story that readers just had to believe it, the Queen refused to give permission for another voyage. Ralegh knew she was still worried about the Spanish and a possible second attempt to invade England. Maybe he should concentrate on dealing with them.

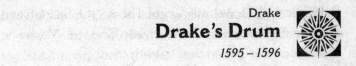

Drake
Drake's Drum
1595 – 1596

DRAKE WASN'T A REFORMED PIRATE by any means. He didn't go to sea himself, but he sent his ships on piratical voyages, and spent quite a bit of time on the Queen's behalf making sure that the other pirates who sailed out of Plymouth didn't keep all the profit for themselves, but sent her a proper share.

He had plenty of work to do, but he wasn't particularly happy doing it. For one thing, his hatred of Spain and the Spanish still boiled over from time to time – we can imagine just how he spoke about them to his guests at dinner at Buckland Abbey. He missed the opportunity to have a go at them, and he also missed going to sea. The war was still going on, though only with occasional fights at sea, and Drake hadn't been called on to take part. In 1593 there had been talk of an expedition to the West Indies, but no one was quite sure how easy or difficult it would be to take any Spanish treasure there. There were stories that the Spanish had very much improved their defences.

But in 1595 Drake and his old friend Sir John Hawkins (their differences had by now been forgotten) were at last told by the Queen to sail against the Spanish, and got together a fleet of 27 ships, led by two splendid vessels, Drake's *Defiance* and Hawkins's *Garland*. They had no trouble finding crews – the chance of sailing again with England's greatest hero was too good to miss, and they set off with between 2,500 and 3,000 recruits, over 1,000 of them soldiers. Drake wanted to go to Panama, where he reckoned there would be rich pickings. The Queen tried to persuade them to stay in European seas, and deal with at least some of the ships she believed were still waiting to attack England. But the chance of great riches and the arguments of the people paying for the expedition, who wanted to be sure of getting their money back, helped change her mind.

Spies soon discovered that "El Draque" was about to sail again with a large fleet, and the Spanish began to panic. They not only sent a warning to the West Indies, but were afraid of an attack on Spain itself – thousands of people actually ran away from Lisbon into the country, thinking that the English would soon land. King Philip commanded Don Pedro Tello to command a fleet of five fast Spanish ships across the Atlantic to collect treasure at Puerto Rico and to help defend the port, and if necessary Panama, against the English.

Now a race was on. The Spanish ships left port on 15 September. Drake and Hawkins needed to get to the West Indies before them. They left Plymouth on 28 August, and reached Las Palmas, in the Spanish Canary Islands, on 27 September – two days before the Spanish ships. Drake tried to take the town but they had seen him coming, and were able to fight him off. While he was hanging about there, the Spanish ships overtook him, and both fleets arrived at the West Indies at about the same time, towards the end of October.

Drake seemed to have lost his touch, and Hawkins was little help; older than Drake, and unwell, he was slow in making decisions, and often made the wrong ones. In early November he died.

Don Pedro had reached Puerto Rico nine days before Drake, and there had been time to strengthen the defences. A thousand men and 70 guns now guarded the treasure, which was in strong boxes ashore. Drake lowered his anchor too close to the shore, and as he was sitting at supper with some friends, a Spanish gun sent a shot clear through his cabin, striking the stool he was sitting on, and injuring two of his guests, one of whom later died. The English ships sailed out of reach, and new plans had to be made hastily.

On the night of 13 November small boats were launched, slid into harbour under cover of darkness, and set fire to most of the Spanish ships. Unfortunately, the

Spaniards were prepared, and managed to put out all the fires except one; the only loss was one of the largest ships, which sank. Before the fires went out, they lit up the whole area, so that the Spanish were able to see the English boats clearly, and fired on them, killing about 50 men.

Drake decided to retreat. An attack on Panama, he thought, would be easier – and there would be more gold. *"I will take you to twenty places far more wealthy,"* he told his officers.

He sailed slowly along the coast of Colombia, burning and looting several towns, none of which turned out to have much treasure. He took a month to reach Nombre de Dios, which he remembered from 20 years earlier. Once again, he took the town easily – indeed the streets were empty as his men marched along them. There was a little gold and silver, but the people of the town had taken their valuables with them when they left.

Now he prepared to take Panama. He sent one of his commanders, Sir Thomas Baskerville, to attack by land; he would bring reinforcements along the river Chagres. His forces fought their way through the forest in rain and mud, then came up against a Spanish fort in a position which was impossible for them to attack successfully. They made an attempt, but after losing 70 men, they turned back to Nombre de Dios.

Drake now decided to give up the whole idea of attacking Panama, and instead to look for new towns where treasure might be found. He burned Nombre de Dios to the ground, and sailed to the island of Escudo, where he set about repairing his ships and trying to re-stock them with food and water.

Soon, his crew realized that their Admiral was no longer to be seen on deck. He was keeping to his cabin, seeing only his officers, friends and servants. The truth was that Escudo was an unhealthy place – several men fell ill while the ship was there – and Drake had caught a fever. On 23 January 1596, he ordered the fleet to sea, steering back towards Nombre de Dios. As they sailed, sickness claimed more victims: the captain of the *Delight* died, and so did the ship's doctor.

Drake was getting weaker and weaker. On 27 January 1596 he dictated some additions to the Will he had made before leaving England, and gave some presents to his servants. Next day, he struggled out of his bunk and ordered his servant to prepare his armour. He wanted, he said, to die as a soldier. But he was too weak, and was helped back to bed. An hour later, at 4 AM on 28 January, he died.

The little fleet gathered around his flagship as trumpets and drums sounded and his body, in a lead coffin, was lowered into the sea at Puerto Bello.

When the news reached England, the death of a hero was mourned. The Spanish were not sorry to see the end of the pirate "El Draque", who in his lifetime had captured more than 500 of their ships, taken so much of their treasure and led the successful fight against the Armada. But they recognized his greatness. He was, one of them said:

very courteous and honourable with those who surrendered, of great humanity and gentleness, virtues which must be praised even in an enemy.

Drake's name is still remembered, and legends have collected around it – the most famous about the drum that went with him on so many of his voyages, and which remains where he put it, hanging at Buckland Abbey. It was said that whenever England was in danger, it would be heard beating. The legend grew and grew. Three centuries later a Victorian poet, Henry Newbolt, put it into verse:

Take my drum to England, hang it by the shore,
Strike it when your powder's runnin' low;
If the Dons sight Devon, I'll quit the port
of Heaven,
An' drum them up the Channel as we drummed
them long ago.

And only 60 years ago, when German bombers destroyed the whole of the centre of Plymouth during the Second World War, people stopped each other in the ruined streets and said: "Did you hear it last night?" They believed that in the pauses between the explosions of the enemy bombs, they had heard the distant sound of Drake's drum, beating, all by itself, as it beat when he went into battle.

The Heart be Right

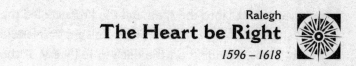

1596 – 1618

ON 3 JUNE 1596, Ralegh put to sea again, as a pirate. With 120 ships, he was going to attack Cadiz, and at one blow strike at the Queen's enemies and, all being well, capture a number of ships and make a good deal of money.

He sailed on the *Warspite*, a brand-new ship of the Queen's with two decks and 40 guns. His great rival Essex was in another ship of the fleet and the two men were on the way to making up their differences. On its way out, the fleet captured a little Irish ship, and the skipper told them that there was a fleet of 50 or 60 merchant ships in Cadiz harbour, with twenty more galleys – and nothing very much to protect them.

"Lord, how every man skipped with joy," wrote Ralegh's doctor, later. Though unlike Drake, who had had many fights at sea, Ralegh had never really been in a sea battle

161

– even when he sailed against the Armada, he had only seen action from a distance. Now was his chance. *"We're going in!"* he shouted. Essex threw his hat in the air (it blew away and fell into the sea), and the *Warspite* led the English ships into Cadiz harbour, with Ralegh, in splendid colourful dress, standing on the deck in full view of the enemy gunners, paying no attention at all to the cannon balls aimed at him. He had all the courage of someone who has never been in a fight, and doesn't know how dangerous it is. He called his trumpeters to the deck, and ordered them to sound a peal of trumpets every time the gunners on shore shot at the ship.

The *Warspite* made straight for the great *San Philip*, but just as they were within reach of each other, a bullet struck Ralegh in the leg, and he had to watch the rest of the battle as two of the biggest Spanish ships exploded and sank. He was taken ashore and carried through the streets on a stretcher, to make sure that the English soldiers and sailors weren't stealing any of the gold and silver or jewels that should rightly belong to him and the Queen.

The merchant ships, with all their rich cargoes, remained untouched further inside the harbour. The Spanish offered a large ransom if the English would let them sail away. Ralegh refused – the treasure was worth far more than what they were offering. But he made a mistake: rather than see the treasure fall into English hands, the Spanish set fire to their ships, and hundreds and thousands of pounds-worth of goods went up in flames.

On his return Elizabeth greeted the wounded Ralegh as a hero and made him again the Captain of her Guard. His secret marriage was forgiven. The Queen now thought of him as one of her chief officers and in July 1597 sent him off with 6,000 soldiers to attack the north coast of Spain and teach the enemy another lesson.

This time, the weather treated Ralegh as it had so often treated Drake. The day after sailing, he woke to find himself separated from the main fleet. As he tried to find it, the storm got worse with waves the size of houses, blinding lightning, deafening thunder. Many of his experienced sailors fell to their knees in panic. He ordered his ship to turn around and run for port. He found when he got to shore that he was the only English ship to have given in to the storm.

Meanwhile, the main fleet had succeeded in reaching the coast of Spain. Ralegh wanted desperately to join them but the wind was against him. At last, the fleet gave up, too – the Spaniards refused to come out and fight. Ralegh suggested to the Queen that they might instead sail for the West Indies, but with the death of Drake fresh in her mind, she refused. She did, however, give permission for a voyage to the Azores as Rear-Admiral to the Earl of Essex. The two men now worked together but didn't really get on, and what success they had was entirely due to Ralegh. He got back to England to find the whole Westcountry in a panic at the news that a new Spanish Armada was making for the coast. He rushed about trying to get the defences in order but then the weather came to the rescue and scattered the Spanish ships.

In 1601, Essex led a plot attempting to overthrow all the Queen's councillors, and tried to raise the city of London against her. He was found guilty of high treason, and condemned to death. As captain of the guard, Ralegh had to be present at his rival's execution. Essex tried to tell him at the last moment that he recognized him as a loyal Englishman, but Ralegh did not hear him. However, those who said he smoked and joked as Essex's head was cut off were wrong – he was sad that a great man had come to such an end.

Ralegh's days as a pirate seemed to be over. All the other great English pirates were dead: Gilbert drowned in 1583; Greville was killed in 1591 and Frobisher in 1594; Hawkins and Drake had died at sea in 1595 and 1596. Ralegh stayed faithfully at Queen Elizabeth's side until her death in 1603. His hatred of the Spanish, who called him Guateral ("Walter-Ral"), did not make him a favourite with King James, who came to the throne after Elizabeth and wished to make peace. Now was the chance for all those who disliked Ralegh to do him harm. They poured into the new King's ear stories about Ralegh's supposed atheism (interested in religion, he had discussed it with others who questioned the existence of God), and suggested that he would not be a friend of James. When the King first met him, he is said to have greeted him with the words: *"I have heard rawly of thee!"*, refering both to how Ralegh's name was pronounced and the fact that Raw meant crude and uncivilized. The King quickly dismissed him from court and virtually threw him out of Durham House, which the Queen had given him.

His enemies triumphed. He was accused of involvement with some Catholics who plotted to capture the King, and could find no way of proving his innocence. He was tried and found guilty. When they heard this, people began to remember all his great deeds, rather than his pride and ambition. Suddenly, public feeling turned in his favour. One man remarked that:

> *...when he saw Sir Walter Ralegh first, he was so led with the common hatred that he would have gone a hundred miles to have seen him hanged, he would, ere they parted, have gone a thousand to save his life...*

Many people agreed that *"never was a man so hated, and so popular, in so short a time"*.

Ralegh was sentenced to death, but because of his fame and his new-found popularity the death sentence was not carried out, and he was imprisoned in the Tower of London. He stayed there for 13 years. While being shut up anywhere for 13 years cannot be pleasant, Ralegh's life was in many ways far from bad. His wife Bess and his ten-year-old son Wat were allowed to live with him in apartments on two floors of the Tower, and his son Carew was actually born there. He had two servants, and his steward came up regularly from Sherborne to take instructions about running the estate.

Ralegh was friendly with the lieutenant of the Tower, Sir George Harvey, and was allowed to take exercise on the narrow terraces on top of the walls. He had a small garden, and a shed in which he experimented with herbs and flowers, producing potions for treating various illnesses. He became very interested in medicine, and treated his servants and several soldiers in the Tower.

Ralegh spent much of his time writing poetry and a long *History of the World*, which included descriptions of some of his own adventures. He wrote this with the help of several assistants, and it starts with the history of Greece, Egypt and the lands of the Bible.

During Ralegh's long imprisonment, King James was unforgiving. He not only refused to pardon him, but actually wrote a short book, *A Counterblast Against Tobacco*, in which he attacked him for picking up the filthy habit of smoking from his friends *"the beastly Indians"*. (Some of those Indians, now Christians and living in England, were among the visitors who were allowed to visit Ralegh during his imprisonment.)

Ralegh persuaded the King to release him so he could lead one more expedition – to Guiana, where he said he would find and run a gold mine he had discovered 20 years earlier. Ralegh was welcomed back to Plymouth, where the Lord Mayor gave him a banquet. He built a fine new ship, the *Destiny*, and set sail with six other vessels. When he got to Guiana, he found no gold, and caught a fever. His son Wat, who had gone with him, took part in an unwise attack on a town on the Orinoco River, where he believed there was gold. He was killed by the Spanish, and the commander of the expedition, Ralegh's friend and lieutenant Lawrence Keymis, committed suicide. Ralegh knew he would have to answer to the King for attacking the Spanish when he had been ordered not to do so. He must have known there would be trouble, and indeed when he struggled back to England, James set up a committee of enquiry that concluded that Ralegh had made up the story about the gold mine. The King made use of the death sentence that had been passed on him 15 years earlier.

On the night before his execution Sir Walter Ralegh wrote on a page of his Bible one of the most famous poems of the time. It ends:

Even such is Time which takes in trust
Our youth, our joys, and all we have,
And pays us but with age and dust,
Who in the dark and silent grave
When we have wandered all our ways
Shuts up the story of our days.
And from which earth and grave and dust
The Lord shall raise me up, I trust.

He was beheaded on 29 October 1618. He went to his death courageously, dressing himself in his best clothes, and shaking hands with those friends who had come to be with him:

I have many, many sins for which to beseech God's pardon. Of a long time my course was a course of vanity. I have been a seafaring man, a soldier, and a courtier, and in the temptations of the least of these there is enough to overthrow a good mind, and a good man.

He felt the blade of the axe with his thumb. *"This is a sharp medicine,"* he said, *"but it is a sure cure for all diseases."* Someone suggested that when he lay down, his head should face east, towards Jerusalem, the holy city. He refused. *"So the heart be right,"* he said, *"it is no matter which way the head lieth"*

The executioner held up his head to show the crowd, but before he could say the words *"Behold the head of a traitor,"* a man in the crowd shouted, *"We have not another such head to be cut off."*

Afterword

WALTER RALEGH AND FRANCIS DRAKE were passionate about two things: Queen Elizabeth and gold. By Elizabeth they also meant England, for in the century in which they lived the Queen was England, in a way that we may find difficult to understand. She was known as Gloriana; she was the glory of the country. She had complete power: she was appointed, it was believed, by God to rule the country, and her word was absolute law. She controlled Parliament, the judges, the Army. She could be forgiving, she could be generous, but she was an absolute dictator. And not only did she have complete power, but she had the glamour that in modern times only a popular hero has – the man who scores the winning goal in a World Cup match, perhaps. And God was unquestionably on her side.

So when you served the Queen, you served England.

Both Drake and Ralegh were happy to do both. They were the Queen's pirates but also England's pirates, for when they brought her gold it was not just because they were happy to make themselves rich, or because she was happy to take her share, but because they were helping her to pay for a Navy to defend her island against the great enemy of them all – Spain.

The two men were very different – and the Queen treated them very differently. Drake was an adventurer, perhaps the cleverest seaman she had, and a man capable of great things. He did not disappoint her, with his amazing round-the-world voyage, and the part he played in the defeat of the Spanish Armada. Ralegh might have been as great an explorer, perhaps as great a seaman as Drake. Unfortunately for him, Elizabeth enjoyed his company too much. If Drake had died it would have been a tragedy for England; if Ralegh had died, it would have been a tragedy for the Queen – so she kept him safely at home. But there he played his part, advising her, looking after the defence of the country.

If these two men were both pirates – and they were – was the Queen a pirate too? You could say so, for when they brought her the treasure that Drake had captured, or which Ralegh had ordered his pirate captains to take, she might tell them off when the Spanish Ambassador was listening – but in private she winked and took her share.

Which of them was the greatest man? It's a question impossible to answer. Drake was a man of action, Ralegh a planner, a thinker (though if the Queen had allowed him, he might have proved as great a seaman and as game a fighter as the other man). Because language has changed, and he used words that are now difficult for us to understand, we find it hard to read Ralegh's poetry and his great *History of the World*; but he was certainly one of the greatest writers of his time (so good that some people have argued that he might have written the plays of Shakespeare!). Though his attempt to establish a colony in Virginia was a failure, he was remembered as its founder – and in time the state was to become the largest in the country, and to supply four of the first five American presidents.

Drake is perhaps the man most people would like to spend an evening with, sitting down at his table in his house in Devon, listening to his stories of his great adventures, his famous drum hanging on the wall behind him.

But nobody interested in England's history can ignore these two very different men who served their Queen and country in different ways, but with one heart.

Further Reading

The best recent biography of Sir Walter Ralegh is by his descendant, Raleigh Trevelyan: *Sir Walter Raleigh* (Penguin, 2003). Shaun McCarthy's *Sir Walter Raleigh* (Heinemann, 2003) is another thorough recent book, and Stephen Coote's *A Play of Passion: the life of Sir Walter Raleigh* (Macmillan, 1993) is also excellent. A.L. Rowse's books about the England of Elizabeth I have many interesting details about Drake, Ralegh and what it was like to be alive at that time.

There are very few good books in print about Francis Drake. The most detailed one is John Sugden's *Sir Francis Drake* (Simon & Schuster, 1992). There is a very good one written specially for young people – Roy Gerrard's *Francis Drake: His Daring Deeds*; it was published in 1989 in America, but copies can be found in UK bookshops. Harry Kelsey's *Sir Francis Drake: the Queen's Pirate* came out in 2000 and is especially good on Drake's life as a pirate. It, too, was published in the USA.

Robert Whiting's *The Enterprise of England* (Sutton, 1988) is a very good and thorough, well-illustrated book about the Spanish Armada.

Acknowledgements

Picture insert

1 Topham Picturepoint
2 Sir Walter Raleigh (1552-1618), Anonymous / Kunsthistorisches Museum, Vienna, Austria, / www.bridgeman.co.uk
3 Topham Picturepoint
4 Mary Evans Picture Library
5 Mary Evans Picture Library
6 The Ark Royal, flagship of Lord Howard of Effingham (1536-1624) at the time of the Armada (engraving) (b&w photo), English School, (16th century) / Private collection, / www.bridgeman.co.uk
7 Topham Picturepoint
8 Defeat of the Spanish Armada, 1588, Anonymous / British Museum, London, UK, / www.bridgeman.co.uk

Index